Weight Training for Life

Second Edition

James L. Hesson

Morton Publishing Company

925 West Kenyon Avenue, Unit 12
Englewood, Colorado 80110

Dedication

To the wind beneath my wings, the creator of all that is.

To Margie, Jennifer, and David, for their love and support.

To all of the teachers, coaches, friends, and colleagues who have shared their time, energy, and knowledge with me.

To my parents, Jack and Gladys Hesson, who taught me the basic values and attitudes that have made all other learning and accomplishment possible.

Printed in the United States of America

10 9 8 7 6 5 4 3 2 1

ISBN: 0-89582-207-5

Preface

Student

Weight Training for Life has been written to you and for you. Learning about weight training by the trial-and-error method can be difficult, embarrassing, and confusing. I hope this book will make learning simple, painless, and easy. Its purpose is to help you build a good foundation of current knowledge and practice in beginning weight training. It does not attempt to include everything to be known about weight training.

This is a book for beginners, not for exercise physiologists or advanced strength athletes. Most of all, this is a book to help you get started weight training for life.

Teacher

Weight Training for Life has been written to help you and to help your students. It does not attempt to cover everything you know about weight training, but it does attempt to organize some basic information that your beginning students should know.

One common challenge for many weight training teachers revolves around time. Answer the following questions quickly.

- Do you have enough class time to tell your students all that you wish you could about weight training?

- Are your students always present, on time, and alert for your weight training lectures?

- Do you have other classes to prepare for?

- Are you paid for talking — or for ensuring that learning takes place?

- Do you ever get bored presenting the same beginning weight training information year after year?

- Have you ever forgotten to mention some basic information you wanted your students to know?

- Could you be more productive if you did not have to repeat the same basic information over and over?

- Would your students learn more effectively if they were required to actively seek information?

- Do you have enough class time to present all the information you want and still have enough exercise time?

- Do you teach more than one weight training class?

- Have you ever noticed how the right tool can help you complete a task easier, faster, and better?

This book is a tool that can help you perform your task of teaching weight training. It can make your performance of this task better and, at the same time, easier. A book will never replace you as a teacher because your role is much more important, dynamic, and complex. Your responsibility is to create a stimulating learning environment, to motivate, to provide direction, and to give feedback.

This tool can be more effective if we work together. As you use the book, let me know how we can improve it to help you and your students. To those of you who used the first edition and sent your suggestions for improvements, you will find most of these in this second edition. Thank you for making this revision possible and for making it better.

Contents

Acknowledgments

I would like to thank everyone who helped make this second edition possible. Special appreciation is given to the following individuals:

Jim Whitehead for his many helpful suggestions.

Clement Jee for his professional photography.

Lindsey Givens, Joey Hart, Scott Mitchell, Kim Moody, Leigh Ann Thornton, and Ken Vanderpool for their time, effort, ideas, encouragement, and patience as models.

Margie Hesson for her professional knowledge and assistance in revising Chapter 14.

Dr. Milton Wilder for years of support, encouragement, and friendship.

Dr. Larry Landis and Sue White for their support and encouragement.

Loren Ferré for "THE CHAIR."

Doug Morton for being an outstanding person as well as an excellent publisher.

What, Who, and Why

WHAT IS WEIGHT TRAINING

Weight training is a form of progressive resistance exercise in which the resistance is gradually increased as your body adapts to the exercise resistance.

Weights of different sizes can be added to, or taken from, the total load to arrive at the correct resistance for each exercise and each muscle group.

Weight training exercises are done for different reasons. The following categories of weight trainers may help you understand why so many different kinds of weight training programs exist.

WHO TRAINS WITH WEIGHTS?

Olympic Lifters

Olympic-style weight lifting is a competitive sport. The objective in olympic-style lifting is to see who can lift the most total weight overhead using two different lifts. The two olympic-style lifts are the snatch and the clean-and-jerk.

The *snatch lift* requires that the weight be lifted in one continuous movement from the floor to a position in which the weight is overhead and both arms are straight. The lifter may drop below the weight to catch it overhead but must rise to a stationary standing position to complete the lift.

Pavel Keznietsov performing the Snatch lift

Photos courtesy of Bruce Klemens

In the *clean-and-jerk lift* the weight must first be brought from the floor to a position on the upper chest and shoulders. Then, from a standing position the weight is thrust overhead to a straight-arm finish.

1   **2**

3   **4**
Yanko Rusev performing the Clean-and-Jerk
Photos courtesy of Bruce Klemens   *(Continued on following page)*

*Yanko Rusev performing
the Clean-and-Jerk*

(continued from previous page)

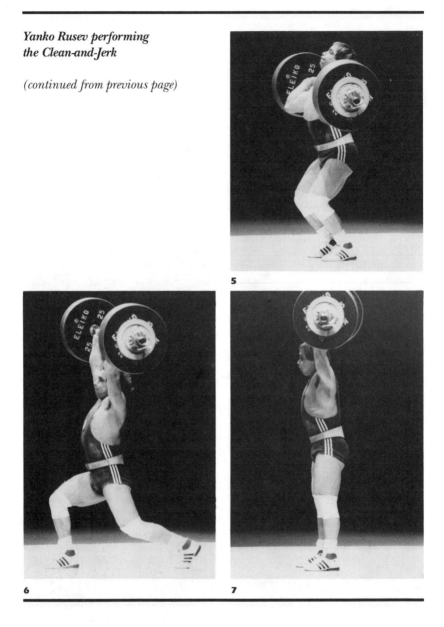

The winner is the individual with the highest total when the snatch and the clean-and-jerk lifts are added together. The competitors are grouped into different body weight classifications so that they are competing against others who are approximately the same size.

Power Lifters

Power lifting is another competitive sport. Power lifters compete in three lifts: the *bench press*, the *squat*, and the *dead lift*. The winner is the lifter with the highest total for the three lifts. These competitors also are grouped by body weight so that they are competing against other lifters who are approximately the same size.

Power Lifter performing the Bench Press

Power Lifter performing the Squat

Power Lifter performing the Dead Lift

Photos courtesy Powerlifting USA Magazine

Body Builders

Body builders participate in competition that is more art than sport. Through weight training they create a living sculpture using the human body as the clay. Body builders attempt to develop maximum muscular size while maintaining a balanced appearance (symmetry) and a high degree of muscular visibility (definition). In this competition the appearance of the body is most important.

Arnold Schwarzenegger   *Dale Adrian*

Photos courtesy of Bruce Klemens

Beauty Pageant Contestants

Most of the women who currently participate in beauty pageants use some form of progressive resistance exercise to prepare for competition. In a recent state beauty competition 38 of the 44 contestants said they use weight training as part of their contest preparation. If 86% of these contestants at the state level of competition use weight training to prepare, the percentage is probably even higher at the national and international levels.

Beauty Contestant Teresa Coghlan

Photo courtesy of Bill Powell

Athletes

Since the rehabilitation work of Dr. Thomas DeLorme following World War II, progressive resistance exercise has gradually gained acceptance by the medical profession and the coaching profession. A dramatic change has taken place during the last 30 years. In the early 1960s most coaches were telling their athletes that they should not lift weights. During the 1970s lifting became more acceptable for athletes. In the 1980s most coaches required their athletes to lift weights.

Most top-level athletes now use some form of weight training to improve their sports performance and to recover from sports injuries. Because skeletal muscles are responsible for all voluntary human movement, athletes who increase the functional ability of their muscular system almost always improve their sports performance.

One relatively new recommendation for athletes is the increased focus on the opposing muscle groups. In the early years of weight training to improve athletic performance, much of the emphasis was placed on the muscles that produce the successful sports movements. Although it did strengthen the desired muscles, and performance did improve, this type of training often created an imbalance of strength surrounding a joint. Occasionally the stronger muscles on one side of the joint overpowered and injured the weaker muscles on the other side of the joint.

Good weight training programs for athletes now include exercises for balanced development to increase performance and reduce the risk of injury.

Patients

Physicians and physical therapists frequently prescribe progressive resistance exercise as a part of the rehabilitation program for people who have been injured. By training with weights, these patients regain strength, muscle size, and functional ability after an injury.

Physical Fitness Enthusiasts

Many people who exercise for health and physical fitness are discovering the benefits of weight training. Most of the people in this category want to look better and feel better.

Weight training and the increase of muscle tissue should be an important part of any fat loss program. Many have overlooked the benefits of weight training for fat loss because of the focus on calories spent during an exercise session. One fairly recent study demonstrated this quite clearly. The researchers concluded that approximately 75 calories per day are used to maintain one pound of muscle and about 3 calories to maintain one pound of body fat. Muscle is active tissue that consumes calories, and fat is inactive tissue that stores calories.

Weight Trainers

Anyone who trains with weights using progressive resistance exercise may be considered a weight trainer. This book has been written primarily for those who are just beginning to lift weights, and for the physical fitness enthusiast, with the hope that if they get off to a good start, they will participate in *Weight Training For Life*.

WHO SHOULD PARTICIPATE IN WEIGHT TRAINING?

Everyone who has a muscular system can benefit from a regular program of progressive resistance exercise.

Women

Is weight training an appropriate activity for girls and women? Absolutely! A strong, trim, muscular, shapely, healthy-looking woman has an irresistible vitality and an aura of vibrant good health. These women are often the center of attention and activity. They frequently are chosen as leaders.

Women who are weak, overfat, and have a soft, flabby appearance are generally not considered very attractive according to current cultural standards. Even though they may be highly capable, they frequently do not get opportunities because of their appearance.

All women achieve increases in muscular strength when they participate in properly planned weight training programs. Most women, however, do not experience much increase in muscular size. This inability to gain muscle size seems to be related to low levels of the hormone testosterone and high levels of the hormone estrogen.

Weight training will not make a woman appear masculine or cause a woman to develop any secondary male characteristics such as a deeper voice, facial hair, or thicker body hair. Because women do show increases in strength with very little increase in muscle size, the result of weight training for women is a strong, firm, shapely, healthy appearance that is unmistakably female.

The location and function of the skeletal muscles is essentially the same in men and women. Research during the last 20 years has indicated that the weight training principles, methods, programs, and exercises that have worked well for men work equally well for women.

Weight training exercises are the same for men and women. Although there are no "men's exercises" or "women's exercises," men and women may choose to concentrate upon developing different body parts and this may affect their selection of exercises.

Men

The benefits of weight training for men have been recognized and accepted longer than they have been for women. Some of the benefits for men are more strength, increased muscle size, greater muscle endurance, improved appearance, higher self-esteem, and better sports performance.

Children

Children can gain important benefits through a carefully planned and closely supervised weight training program. Those who participate in weight training can gain strength, heighten their self-image, increase their level of physical fitness, improve their sports performance, and possibly reduce their risk of youth sport injury.

The risk of injury from weight training during participation in a carefully planned and closely supervised weight training program for children is low. The injuries that have been reported usually have occurred during improperly performed overhead lifts. Too much weight, improper technique, poorly planned programs, and a lack of supervision may have been contributing factors.

Those who are responsible for planning and supervising weight training programs for children must be trained and qualified in this area. Each exercise has to be taught and demonstrated correctly, along with the spotting techniques for that exercise. The young weight trainer should not be allowed to train alone without proper supervision and a trained spotter.

The training area should be clean, bright, attractive, safe, and large enough to perform each lift safely. It should not be dark, dirty, dingy, cluttered, and small.

Training programs for children should focus on all-around physical development, not just strength training. Strength is only one aspect of physical development.

Children should train with moderate to light weights that can be handled for fairly high repetitions. The National Strength and Conditioning Association recommends six to 15 repetitions in each set. This means that a child should not be allowed to lift a weight unless he or she can complete at least six correct repetitions with that weight. Children should not attempt one-repetition maximum lifts.

Children should be allowed to participate in weight training voluntarily. If young children are forced to participate in weight training, they are likely to develop a negative attitude toward this beneficial activity. If they develop a negative attitude, they probably will not participate in *Weight Training for Life*.

After puberty and during adolescence, as hormone changes occur, children begin to experience greater physical changes as a result of a weight training program. During this time strict exercise form should be maintained, and close qualified adult supervision is critical. Boys at this age seem to have an overwhelming urge to find out who can lift the most weight one time. Of course, what they most often find out is how much they cannot lift one time. The risk of injury is too high.

As young people near full growth and full physical maturity, weight training can have its most dramatic positive effects on physical performance, appearance, and self-confidence. This is a time when they can handle heavier exercise loads and more intense exercise programs. To maximize safety and progress, however, the emphasis must always remain on correct exercise technique. Many young men resort to poor exercise technique to move a heavier weight. This obviously can result in injury. Weight training exercises performed correctly rarely result in injury.

Adults

During the aging process, strength and muscle mass decline. How much of this decrease is a result of biological aging and how much is a result of a sedentary lifestyle? Very little of the decline in strength during the adult years is a result of natural aging. Societies that have a high degree of technology and automation reveal a much greater loss of strength and mobility with aging, because of inactivity and a failure to maintain the muscular system.

Many individuals in these "wage-earning adult years" think they do not have time for weight training, when in fact weight training is an efficient form of exercise. With weight training, a muscle group can be isolated and worked very hard in an extremely short time. A stimulus strong enough to maintain strength, or to cause a gain in the strength of a muscle group, may be achieved in about one minute with some weight training programs. This is a greater strength gain stimulus than the same muscle group would achieve in hours of participating in most adult recreational activities.

All of the major muscles in the body can be exercised in 15 to 20 minutes. If such a weight training program is performed two or three times each week, that would be an investment of 30 to 60 minutes a week. Each week has 168 hours, and you can maintain your strength during your adult years by investing one of those hours in weight training. If your time for exercise is limited, weight training is one of the fastest ways to maintain or increase the functioning of your muscular system. It is important for adults to continue *Weight Training for Life.*

Older Adults

At what age should adults stop weight training? Never! Humans should not use age as an excuse to stop weight training. Some older adults may be advised by their physicians to stop weight training because of medical problems, but as long as there is no medical reason to quit, there is no reason to stop weight training at any certain age. Weight training programs, however, do have to be modified with age.

Sometime in their 60s, 70s, 80s, or 90s, most older adults experience a more rapid decline in physical performance. It has been difficult to determine how much of this decline is due to the decrease in physical activity that often accompanies retirement and how much relates to a person's decision that it is time to get old and to act old.

In either case, older adults must maintain their muscular system if they wish to retain their freedom and their mobility. Enjoyment is often closely related to physical mobility at all ages, but the lack of enjoyment becomes more obvious with older adults who have lost their ability to get around on their own. Therefore, older adults should participate in *Weight Training for Life*.

Everyone

Weight training is an efficient form of exercise to develop and maintain your muscular system. Though your goals and training programs will change as you progress through life, weight training is a valuable lifetime activity that you should continue. Everyone should participate in some form of *Weight Training for Life*.

WHAT CONTRIBUTIONS CAN WEIGHT TRAINING MAKE TO TOTAL PERSONAL DEVELOPMENT?

Total personal development includes physical, mental, social, emotional, and spiritual development. Weight training can contribute to all of these areas of personal development in some way.

Physical

Weight training makes its most obvious contributions in the area of physical development. All of the following can be improved with a well planned weight training program:

- muscle strength

- tendon strength
- ligament strength
- bone strength
- muscle size for men
- muscle tone for women
- appearance
- posture
- flexibility
- metabolism
- joint stability
- muscle endurance
- power
- sports performance
- lean body mass
- physical fitness
- health

Weight training is a lifetime activity that can help you to maintain fitness, reduce body fat, and reduce the risk and rate of injury.

Mental

A successful weight training program requires an understanding of how the body functions and how it responds to exercise, intelligent planning, consistent self-discipline, continual analysis, and insightful problem solving.

Social

When weight training is performed with others, positive social qualities can be developed. Sharing, caring, encouraging, and helping are among the positive social behaviors that should occur during weight training workouts. These workouts provide a time to participate with others in an activity that produces positive results for all participants. In contrast to many recreational games, which must result in a winner and a loser, everyone is a winner in weight training.

Weight training provides a common activity in which to participate and a common topic to discuss, as well as a time to be together. It can be an excellent activity for family members or friends because everyone can be together, yet all can perform their own individual training program at their own level without interfering with the progress of anyone else.

A good weight training program includes the achievement of goals. To share your goals with others and to see and help others achieve their goals, is very rewarding. A bond often develops among those who do the difficult exercises together. Weight training is an activity that can be done alone, with one training partner, or with a group.

Emotional

Weight training can help a person release emotional stress and tension. A measurable decrease in neuromuscular tension occurs following a weight training session. It also provides an opportunity to release anger and frustration in a socially acceptable and healthy manner — intense physical activity that is not directed at another person.

Because weight training involves overcoming physical difficulties during each training session, some regular participants seem to adopt a more objective and positive approach to other obstacles and difficulties in their lives. This produces greater emotional stability.

Measurable and noticeable changes in physical appearance result from a well planned weight training program. The increased muscle size for men and muscle tone for women create a firm, shapely appearance that is appropriate for each gender. That firm, trim, athletic look can never be achieved by diet alone. Usually, posture also improves. These physical improvements tend to be accompanied by an enhanced self-image and greater self-esteem. Those who lift weights often look better and feel better about themselves.

Spiritual

The spirit refers to the soul or the life force within each living human. It is one of those intangible and invisible things in life that cannot be measured or adequately described. Yet, somehow you know it is there. Sometimes it seems that those who increase the strength of their body and their mind also become stronger in spirit. They seem to have a greater resiliency, a greater life force, a stronger spirit.

It has been said that many can "talk the talk" but few can "walk the walk". Weight training can help you become a "can do" person instead of a "can't do" person.

2

Common Questions

IF I BUILD UP A LOT OF MUSCLE, WILL IT TURN TO FAT WHEN I STOP WEIGHT TRAINING?

No. Muscle tissue and fat tissue are two distinctly different kinds of tissue in the human body, and muscle tissue cannot become fat tissue. But if you stop training, you can accumulate more body fat.

Muscle tissue adapts to the demands placed upon it. When you stop training, your muscles will adapt to the new demand. If the new demand is much lower than it was before, the muscles will respond by getting smaller and weaker (*atrophy*). If you continue eating like you did when you were training hard every day, the extra calories will now be stored as body fat. Even if you manage to stay at the same body weight, you will have less muscle and more fat, leaving you with the outward appearance that your muscles have turned to fat. Because fat tissue is not as dense as muscle tissue, you can also expect to gain inches in your body circumference measurements.

To make matters worse, as you lose metabolically active muscle tissue, your ability to use calories is reduced. Muscle cells are active calorie-burning cells. As these calorie-burning cells atrophy, your metabolic rate slows down and you need even fewer calories than before. To think you can maintain a trim, muscular, shapely appearance by diet alone, is foolish. Are you beginning to realize the importance of *Weight Training for Life?*

WILL WEIGHT TRAINING MAKE A WOMAN LOOK LIKE A MAN?

No. Hormones, not weight training, determine if a woman appears more masculine or feminine.Women who train with weights can develop a healthy shapely, trim female figure. In fact, *most* of the women who are now competing in beauty pageants use some form of progressive resistance exercise to prepare for competition. Also, many of the most attractive female movie stars exercise with weights.

WILL WEIGHT TRAINING MAKE ME MUSCLE-BOUND?

No. If you follow correct weight training principles, weight training will not make you muscle-bound. Muscle-bound refers to a condition in which a person has a limited range of joint motion. Correct weight training principles include training each muscle through a full range of motion. Each muscle should be exercised from full extension to full contraction. Also, the opposing muscles should receive an equal amount of exercise so the muscles on one side of a joint do not develop more than those on the other side. When these principles are followed, the weight trainer will generally experience an increase, rather than a decrease, in flexibility and joint mobility. The United States has many more "fat-bound" people than "muscle-bound" people.

Athletes may become muscle-bound as a result of the un-balanced muscular development induced by many sports. Also, when athletes train with weights to improve their sports performance, they typically train only those muscles that are already over-developed, and ignore balanced development. The result is that athletes sometimes see weight training as the reason for their muscle-bound condition when in fact their condition is the result of a poorly planned weight training program.

The gymnast is probably one of the best examples of a high level of strength development accompanied by a high level of flexibility. Research also has shown that olympic weight lifters are among the most flexible athletes at the Olympic Games.

WILL WEIGHT TRAINING "SHAPE UP" A CERTAIN PART OF MY BODY?

Yes and no. Exercises for a specific body part will firm up weak, sagging muscles and may result in a trimmer appearance but will not effectively reduce excess body fat stored in that area.

The idea of losing body fat from a specific body part is known as *spot reduction*. Examples of spot reduction are sit-ups to lose fat from the abdomen and hip extensions to lose fat from the hips. Unfortunately, the research to date indicates that spot reduction does not work. To lose fat from a specific area requires total body fat reduction. This is best accomplished by reducing caloric intake (eating) and increasing caloric expenditure (exercise). The best type of exercise to lose body fat is one that uses the large muscles of the body in a rhythmic and continuous manner. Good examples of exercises for the loss of excess body fat are walking, jogging, bicycling, and swimming.

Of course, weight training will build muscle tissue. This increase in muscle tissue should help with fat loss by giving you more active muscle tissue that is capable of using calories and by raising your resting metabolic rate so that you will use more calories even when you are resting. If you want to shape up your body, consider *Weight Training for Life*.

IS WEIGHT TRAINING BAD FOR MY HEART?

No. There is no indication that weight training is harmful to the normal, healthy heart. In fact, the results of research studies indicate that the opposite is true. Studies have shown an increase in the size and strength of the heart as result of a weight training program.

WILL WEIGHT TRAINING MAKE ME SLOWER?

No. Coaches used to tell their athletes not to lift weights because it would make them slower. The research in this area, however, indicates that the opposite is true: Weight training increases speed. Muscle contraction is responsible for human movement. With weight training, strength increases more than body weight, so the individual will have a greater strength-to-weight ratio. A stronger muscle can move a body part faster. Muscular weakness and excess body fat will make you slower.

WILL WEIGHT TRAINING DAMAGE MY JOINTS?

No. Weight training exercises done correctly will increase joint strength. Exercises should be performed in a smooth, continuous manner.

Weight training exercises performed improperly could damage your joints. Jerking, throwing, and dropping weights should be avoided because these incorrect lifting techniques may result in injury.

DOES WEIGHT TRAINING REQUIRE HOURS AND HOURS OF TRAINING EACH WEEK?

No. Weight training is one of the most efficient forms of exercise. All of the major muscle groups in the body can be trained in 15 minutes. The program should be repeated two or three times each week. You will not find many effective exercise programs that are faster than that!

The amount of time you need to spend training with weights will be directly related to the goals you set for yourself. Body builders, olympic lifters, and power lifters do spend many hours each week training with weights; however, that is what they enjoy doing, and they have set some very high goals.

WILL WEIGHT TRAINING RUIN MY COORDINATION?

No. There is some adjustment to an increase in strength, but most people can make this minor adjustment with no problem because strength gain is relatively slow. For the athlete in a sport in which "touch" or "timing" is critical, it is best to increase strength during the off season and maintain that strength level through the competitive season. For the weak and untrained individual, weight training may improve coordination.

WILL WEIGHT TRAINING STUNT MY GROWTH?

No. Weight training does not seem to have any effect on height. Height is determined genetically. Weight training does result in stronger bones, ligaments, and tendons. Sometimes shorter men and thinner men train with weights to develop a more muscular or "masculine" appearance. A man may appear to be more muscular because he is short, or he may train to be more muscular because he is short, but weight training was not what made him short.

CAN I GAIN AS MUCH STRENGTH FROM SPORTS PARTICIPATION AS I CAN FROM WEIGHT TRAINING?

No. Most sports do not provide the right type, intensity, duration, or frequency of exercise to increase strength. Weight training can produce a strength gain stimulus in one minute that is greater than a muscle would receive in hours of participation in most recreational activities.

Many recreational sports injuries are the result of placing an unfit body in a competitive situation. You should gain strength to participate in sports instead of participating in sports to gain strength.

COULD HEAVY LIFTING CAUSE A HERNIA?

Yes. A hernia, or a rupture in the abdominopelvic cavity, occurs when any of the internal organs is pushed through the wall that surrounds it. If you hold your breath and strain to lift an object that is too heavy, the pressure in the abdominal cavity increases to a high level and may result in a hernia. This often happens to individuals who do not train on a regular basis and do not know their own capability or correct lifting technique. The unfit person moving furniture is a classic example.

It is possible, but highly unlikely, that a hernia could be caused during a well planned weight training program using correct lifting techniques. Correct weight training procedures require that you never hold your breath while lifting. Exhaling as you exert force is generally best. In weight training you should learn about, and practice, correct lifting mechanics. These two factors, along with knowing how much weight you can safely lift, should reduce your risk of experiencing a hernia while weight training.

CAN WEIGHT TRAINING DEVELOP TOTAL HEALTH-RELATED PHYSICAL FITNESS?

Yes. It is possible for a well planned circuit weight training program to develop all aspects of health-related physical fitness. Total health-related physical fitness involves the development of cardiovascular endurance, strength, muscular endurance, flexibility, and control of body fat. Most weight training programs, however, can best develop strength or muscular endurance. More effective ways are available to develop the other aspects of physical fitness.

WHEN IS A PERSON TOO OLD TO START WEIGHT TRAINING?

Never. A person is never too old to start a sensible weight training program. Each training program should be planned for a specific individual. Some people may be too unhealthy, but never too old. Weight training can be beneficial for anyone who has a muscular system to maintain. Your goals, training programs, and results will be different, but weight training can be beneficial at any age.

3

Muscle Structure and Function

GENERAL INFORMATION ABOUT YOUR MUSCULAR SYSTEM

Your body has approximately 600 muscles, making up about 50% of your total body weight. Skeletal muscles account for about 40% of your total body weight, and the other 10% is primarily involuntary muscle of the circulatory and digestive system. Although muscles vary a great deal in size, shape, arrangement of fibers, and internal characteristics, they all perform the same general function — which is to provide movement. It is difficult to overemphasize the importance of muscle tissue. All human movement is the result of muscle contraction.

CHARACTERISTICS OF MUSCLE TISSUE

Extensibility

Extensibility refers to the ability of muscle tissue to be stretched. If muscle tissue could not stretch, you would not have the mobility or range of motion that you now have.

Elasticity

Elasticity is the ability of muscle tissue to return to its normal resting length and shape after being stretched. If muscle tissue did

21

not have elasticity, it would remain at whatever length you stretched it to.

Excitability

Excitability refers to the ability of muscle tissue to receive a stimulus from the nervous system.

Contractility

Contractility is the quality that really sets muscle tissue apart. When a stimulus is received, muscle tissue can contract, or shorten.

These four characteristics combine to make muscle tissue a very special kind of tissue. Muscle tissue is responsible for every movement your body makes.

TYPES OF MUSCLE TISSUE

Cardiac

Cardiac muscle is found only in the heart and is considered involuntary muscle because a person cannot consciously contract the heart muscle.

Smooth

Smooth muscle primarily lines hollow internal structures such as blood vessels and the digestive tract. Smooth muscle also is considered involuntary because its contraction and relaxation are automatic functions and not the result of conscious voluntary control.

Skeletal

The primary focus of this book is the development of skeletal muscle, which is attached to the bones or skeletal system. Skeletal muscle is voluntary muscle, and the contraction of skeletal muscle is a result of conscious voluntary control.

THE SKELETAL SYSTEM AS A LEVER SYSTEM

The three classifications of levers are: first class, second class, and third class. All three types of levers are found in the skeletal system of the human body. Not only are there three types of levers, but there are also six different kinds of joints that are considered freely movable. The result is a wide range of human movement possibilities. The movements that take place are the result of muscle tissue pulling on separate bones or tissues across a joint. Some joints, such as the ball-and-socket joint of the shoulder, have a wide range of movement possibilities that may be strengthened, whereas others, such as the hinge joint of the elbow, are limited to two movements, flexion and extension.

THE STRUCTURE OF SKELETAL MUSCLE

A complete muscle has connective tissue at each end, which attaches muscle to bone. See Figure 3.1. This connective tissue is

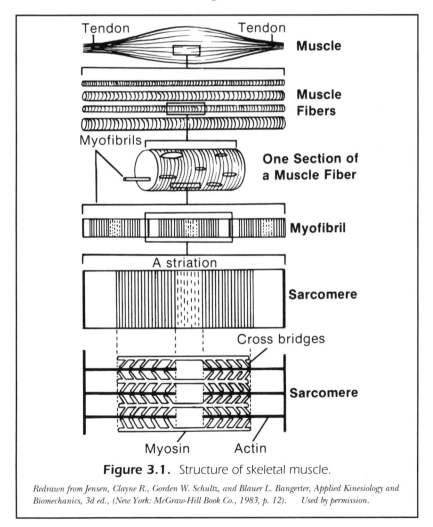

Figure 3.1. Structure of skeletal muscle.

Redrawn from Jensen, Clayne R., Gorden W. Schultz, and Blauer L. Bangerter, Applied Kinesiology and Biomechanics, 3d ed., (New York: McGraw-Hill Book Co., 1983, p. 12). Used by permission.

called a *tendon*. The tendon is continuous with connective tissue that encloses the muscle tissue.

Within the muscle are bundles of *muscle fibers* (cells). Skeletal muscle fibers (cells) are generally long and relatively small in diameter. See Figure 3.1.

Within each muscle fiber are long thread-like structures called *myofibrils*. These myofibrils run lengthwise through the muscle fiber. Each myofibril consists of many sarcomeres attached end to end. See Figure 3.1. The *sarcomere* is the basic contractile unit of skeletal muscle tissue. See Figure 3.1. Within the sarcomere are *myofilaments*. The thinner myofilaments are called *actin* and the thicker myofilaments are called *myosin*. According to the sliding filament theory of muscle contraction, the myosin filaments have cross bridges that contact the actin filaments. The actin and myosin filaments do not change in length, but the myosin cross bridges pull the actin filaments toward the center. Because the actin filaments are attached to the ends of the sarcomere, the sarcomere becomes shorter in length as the filaments are pulled toward the center.

MUSCLE CONTRACTION AND EXERCISE MOVEMENTS

Muscle tissue can only contract or relax. Therefore, muscle can only pull on bones or stop pulling on bones. Muscle tissue cannot push. In some exercises an object, such as a barbell, is pushed away from the body. This is accomplished by muscles pulling on bones and causing the joints to extend. In other pulling exercises muscles pull on bones to pull a weight toward the body. All exercises involve muscles pulling on bones across a joint. Again, muscle tissue can only pull on bones. The movement that takes place depends upon the structure of the joint and the muscle attachments involved. See Figure 3.2.

Isometric Contraction

Iso refers to equal, and *metric* refers to length or measure; therefore, an isometric contraction is one in which the muscle maintains an equal length. This occurs when contracting a muscle and creating a force against an immovable object. The muscle contracts and tries to shorten but cannot overcome the resistance.

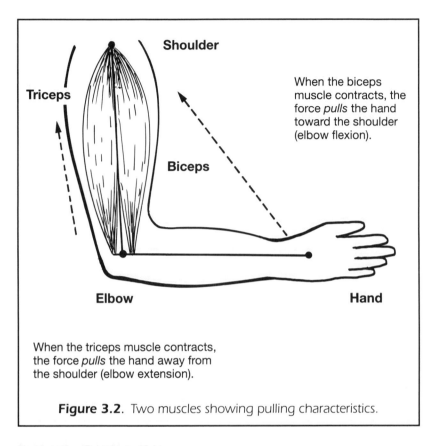

Shoulder

Triceps

When the biceps muscle contracts, the force *pulls* the hand toward the shoulder (elbow flexion).

Biceps

Elbow   **Hand**

When the triceps muscle contracts, the force *pulls* the hand away from the shoulder (elbow extension).

Figure 3.2. Two muscles showing pulling characteristics.

Isotonic Contraction

Iso refers to equal or constant, and *tonic* refers to tone or tension; therefore, an isotonic exercise is one in which movement occurs but muscle tension remains about the same. This occurs in most weight training exercise movements.

Concentric Contraction

A concentric contraction is a shortening contraction in which the muscle becomes shorter and overcomes the resistance.

Eccentric Contraction

An eccentric contraction is a lengthening contraction in which the muscle contracts and tries to shorten but is overcome by the resistance.

Isokinetic Contraction

Iso refers to equal or constant, and *kinetic* refers to motion; therefore, a true isokinetic contraction is a constant speed contraction. The speed is set on the exercise device so that the muscle can contract at 100% throughout the full range of motion without any acceleration occurring.

MOTOR UNIT

A motor nerve is a nerve that comes from the brain or spinal cord and causes something to happen, contrasted with a sensory nerve, which takes information to the central nervous system. A motor unit consists of a single motor nerve and all the muscle fibers it sends impulses to. Although a motor nerve is connected to many muscle fibers, each muscle fiber is controlled by only one motor nerve. A motor nerve that is responsible for very fine movement may be connected to only 10 muscle fibers, such as those responsible for eye movements. A motor nerve responsible for large or heavy human movements may be connected to 500 muscle fibers, such as those responsible for hip extension.

The All or None Principle

A muscle fiber contracts completely or not at all. If a stimulus for contraction is below the threshold value, no contraction occurs. If the stimulus is above the threshold value, complete contraction occurs. All of the muscle fibers in a motor unit contract completely or not at all.

Recruitment

Hundreds of motor units are contained in each muscle. The force a muscle exerts is determined primarily by the size and number of motor units recruited for a task.

MUSCLE ATROPHY AND HYPERTROPHY

Muscles that are not used will shrink in size (atrophy) to a size that is adequate for the demands placed upon them. A good example of muscle atrophy occurs with a broken leg or arm that is immobilized in a cast during the healing process. When the cast is removed, that arm or leg is much smaller than the active limb. The same thing happens to people who do not train their muscular system; however, the reduction in size occurs in both limbs and is so gradual that it often goes unnoticed.

The opposite is also generally true: Muscles that are forced to work harder than normal generally hypertrophy, or increase in size. This muscle growth is much more visible and more pronounced in men than it is in women. The reason for this greater increase in muscle size in men is thought to be related to the hormone testosterone.

As your curiosity about muscle structure and function increases, you may want to refer to current human anatomy, human physiology, and exercise physiology textbooks for detailed information.

4

Warm-Up, Flexibility, and Stretching

WARM-UP

Before participating in vigorous physical activity, most adults prefer to warm up. Warm-up activities usually consist of light muscular activity and some kind of light stretching movements. It is reasonable to believe that a warm-up may improve performance and reduce the risk of injury. Though both of these beliefs are difficult to prove, using the scientific method of investigation, warming up before participating in vigorous physical activity is still generally considered wise.

One effective way to warm up for weight training is to perform light warm-up sets for each exercise before progressing to heavier sets for that same exercise. For example, if your weight training program begins with bench press, you would perform one or more sets of bench press slowly and smoothly to stretch and warm up the exact muscles and joints that will be used when you perform heavier sets of this same exercise. Almost all olympic lifters, power lifters, body builders, and athletes warm up for heavy exercise in this manner. This method of warm-up seems to be beneficial for mental preparation as well as physical preparation to exert greater effort in later, heavier sets of an exercise.

Another effective way to warm up your body is to perform some type of cardiovascular endurance activity before training with weights — activities such as walking, jogging, and bicycling.

FLEXIBILITY

Flexibility refers to the range of motion available in a joint. It is specific to each joint and each direction in which the joint allows movement. Therefore, a person might be flexible in shoulder joint movements and tight in hip joint movements. An individual also could be flexible in hip joint flexion but tight in hip joint extension or hyperextension.

Correct weight training should increase your flexibility. Correct weight training consists of (a) exercise through a full range of joint motion in a smooth and continuous manner, and (b) a balanced program of exercises for all opposing muscle groups that surround a joint.

Those who do not perform any exercise, those who participate in only one sport, and athletes who have trained with weights but have used partial movements or have neglected to develop opposing muscle groups are frequently less flexible than those who train correctly with weights.

How much flexibility is enough? No absolute measurable standard exists for how much flexibility you need to be healthy. In general, a joint should move freely in all of the directions appropriate for that joint.

Is more flexibility better? Not always. There is a trade-off between flexibility and joint stability. If a joint has too much flexibility, it is less stable and the individual is more likely to experience dislocation-type injuries. On the other hand, if a joint has too little flexibility, it is very stable but the individual is more likely to experience soft tissue injuries to the muscles, tendons, and ligaments.

Weight training can be an ideal exercise to arrive at the optimal amount of flexibility because each joint should be moved through a full range of motion, which increases or maintains flexibility, and all of the muscles, tendons, and ligaments that surround and support a joint are strengthened by the progressive resistance. One result of correct weight training should be strong, flexible joints.

Equipment can make a difference. Dumbbells generally allow the greatest range of motion and therefore may contribute more to flexibility. The range of motion of some exercise machines is not as great as that of the individual using the machine. In this case, the individual will not increase flexibility when exercising on that particular machine.

STRETCHING

Stretching is a type of exercise used to increase flexibility. The range of motion of a joint usually is restricted by the soft tissue surrounding it — muscles, tendons, and ligaments. Therefore, stretching exercises should gently stretch these soft tissues without damaging them or the joint. The following guidelines have been proven to meet this criteria:

Type:	Static stretch
Intensity:	Moderate discomfort
Duration:	10- to 30-second hold
	1 to 3 repetitions
Frequency:	3 to 7 days per week

Type (static stretch)

Stretching exercises can be performed in many different ways. Static stretch is a method of stretching in which the bones of a joint are moved to the point where the soft tissues surrounding the joint restrict further movement. These soft tissues (muscle, tendon, ligament, joint capsule) then are gently stretched and held in this stretched position for a period of time.

Six reasons for recommending static stretch are:

- It is an effective way to increase flexibility.
- The risk of injury is low.
- It is easy to learn.
- You can stretch alone.
- Static stretch relieves some types of muscle soreness.
- Performed correctly, static stretch does not cause muscle soreness (some other methods of stretching can cause muscle soreness.)

Intensity (moderate discomfort)

To be effective in increasing flexibility, the soft connective tissue surrounding a joint has to be stretched to a position about 10% beyond it's normal length. Because this is difficult to measure, we have a built-in mechanism for judging the intensity of a static stretching exercise: pain receptors.

When you are stretching at the correct intensity, you will experience moderate discomfort in the muscles being stretched. If the muscles do not have enough tension for you to tell which muscles are being stretched, you have not stretched far enough. On the other hand, if you experience pain while stretching, you are going too far and could injure yourself.

Duration (10 to 30 seconds and 1 to 3 repetitions)

When you are performing static stretching exercises, you should hold a static position at an intensity of moderate discomfort for at least 10 seconds but not more than 30 seconds. You should perform each stretching exercise at least once. For the average person, who is stretching for physical fitness, performing each stretching exercise more than three times is not necessary.

Frequency (3 to 7 days per week)

To be most effective in increasing flexibility, static stretching exercises should be repeated at least three days per week. Static stretching exercises can be performed up to seven days per week.

Joints to Stretch

A stretching exercise can be designed for every muscle and every joint in your body; however, stretching the following major areas is more practical: shoulders, wrists, hips, knees, and ankles. Each of these joints is stretched in each major direction that it can move, and held in that position for 10 to 30 seconds. Your weight training instructor can give you advice on safe stretching exercises.

Recently, many good stretching exercises have been labeled as potentially harmful. Generally, it is not the exercise itself but, instead, the way the exercise is performed that makes it harmful.

You should always be careful when stretching so the exercises produce flexibility and not injury.

When to Stretch

Many individuals feel better if they stretch their muscles and joints prior to more vigorous exercise such as weight training. This stretching may help prevent exercise injuries and may improve performance, though little conclusive research evidence is available to support either of these common beliefs.

Results of some research have indicated that vigorous stretching of cold muscles may be harmful. Therefore, any stretching before warming the muscles should be done carefully. Stretching cold muscles should be done through light, gentle stretching exercises designed to "loosen up" the movements of those joints.

Vigorous stretching to increase flexibility should be done only after the muscles and joints are thoroughly warmed up. One good time to do this type of stretching is immediately after your weight training workout.

5

Guidelines for Performing a Weight Training Exercise

Follow these guidelines for performing a weight training exercise to maximize your weight training progress and your safety.

STRICT EXERCISE FORM

By maintaining strict exercise form, you will keep the load on the muscles that the exercise was designed to develop. When you do not maintain strict exercise form, you will reduce the load on the muscles you are trying to develop and will increase your risk of injury.

SMOOTH MOVEMENT

Weight training exercises should be performed in a smooth, continuous movement. Some exercises are done faster than others, and some involve acceleration, but they should all be smooth. This allows the muscle to apply force to the resistance throughout the full range of motion. The purpose of weight training is to build healthy muscle tissue, not to tear it apart.

FULL RANGE OF MOTION

Whenever possible, a muscle should be exercised from full extension to full contraction and back to full extension. This results in strength gains throughout the complete range of motion of the muscle in the concentric phase (shortening) and the eccentric phase (lengthening). It also helps prevent a loss of flexibility.

CONCENTRIC PHASE

In the concentric phase of an exercise, the muscle contraction overcomes the resistance. This causes the muscle to get shorter as the weight is raised. For most exercises this concentric phase should take one to two seconds.

ECCENTRIC PHASE

During the eccentric phase of an exercise, the same muscles that raised the weight now lower the weight. In this phase the weight is allowed to overcome the force of muscle contraction. Therefore, even though the muscle is contracting and trying to shorten, it is being lengthened by the pull of the resistance. Eccentric contractions allow us to lower objects in a smooth controlled manner. Weights should almost always be lowered smoothly and continuously.

The eccentric phase of an exercise should take at least as long as the concentric phase (one to two seconds), and sometimes up to twice as long (two to four seconds). Because the same muscles are working to raise and lower the weight, only half an exercise would be completed by allowing the weight to drop after it has been lifted.

Among those who gain the least from a weight training exercise are those who throw the weight upward using poor exercise form, incorrect muscle groups, and momentum. Then, once the weight has been raised, they allow it to drop back to the starting position. Those individuals may lift more weight, but they receive less benefit from the exercise and have a much greater risk of injury.

BREATHING

A good general rule for breathing during weight training exercises is to exhale during the greatest exertion — usually the

concentric phase of the exercise (lifting) — and inhale when lowering (the eccentric phase). One exception to this rule occurs when performing overhead pressing movements. Some weight trainers are more comfortable inhaling as they press the weight overhead and exhaling as they lower it.

Proper breathing is an important part of correct exercise technique. It should be practiced while new exercises are being learned with lighter weights. A breathing pattern should be learned with each exercise. There is some room for individual differences and preferences.

The one thing that should be avoided is holding your breath while straining to lift a heavy weight. This produces a great deal of pressure inside the chest cavity and the abdominal cavity, making it difficult, or even impossible, for the blood in the veins to return to the heart. The sudden high pressure caused by straining to lift a heavy weight while holding your breath could cause dizziness, a blackout, a stroke, a heart attack, or a hernia. Although events such as these are extremely rare in weight trainers, the possibility of their occurrence should emphasize the importance of learning to breathe properly during the exercises.

CONCENTRATION

Full attention should be focused on the muscles that are moving the weight. This concentration should be maintained on every repetition, and throughout every set, to gain the maximum benefit from the exercise. Weight trainers should not let their mind wander while performing a weight training exercise.

Willie Brown doing Concentration Curls.

Photo courtesy of Bill Powell

ISOLATED INTENSITY

Isolated intensity is closely related to concentration and getting the greatest benefit from weight training in the least amount of exercise time. Isolated intensity means focusing on a muscle, or group of muscles, that you wish to develop and forcing the muscle to work very hard. As you advance in your muscle training, you will learn how to force a muscle to work to temporary failure. This is beyond the point where you would like to quit and to the point where the muscle cannot perform the task. It is very intense exercise for an isolated group of muscles and is much more effective in producing gains than easier sets that are stopped when they begin to get difficult.

Working muscles to the point of temporary muscular failure is not recommended for beginning weight trainers. It can result in extreme muscle soreness and serious injury.

6

Beginning and Lifetime Weight Training Programs

MACHINES AND FREE WEIGHTS

Two beginning weight training programs are presented in this chapter. One program uses machines or weight-stack equipment. The other program consists of barbell and dumbbell exercises. These have been selected because they represent the weight training equipment most commonly available to beginners.

Machines have some advantages over barbells and dumbbells:

- They are generally safer because the weights cannot fall on you.

- Changing from one weight to another is usually faster because you only need to move a selector pin.

- The exercise movement is easier and faster to learn because it is limited by the machine.

Free weights (barbells and dumbbells) have some advantages over weight machines:

- They offer a greater variety of exercise movements because movement is not restricted by machine design.

- They are available at a much lower cost than most exercise machines.

- They are easier to move from one location to another.

- They are the right size for everyone. One size fits all.
- Many additional stabilizing and assisting muscles must be used to hold your body in the correct exercise position and to keep the weight moving along the correct path.

MEDICAL CLEARANCE

Getting a complete physical examination before starting any new exercise program is a good idea. The physician should be told that you want to start a weight training program and asked if there is any reason that you should not. Medical clearance becomes increasingly important as you get older, if you are overweight, or if you have not participated in a physical training program for a long time.

CLOTHING

Clothing for weight training should allow freedom of movement during all exercises through a complete range of motion. When the weather or the gym is warm, most weight trainers wear gym shorts, a t-shirt or tank-top, socks and shoes. When the training environment is cold, a cotton sweat-suit is usually worn over the shorts and shirt. Cotton material absorbs perspiration better than most synthetic materials and tends to be more comfortable during exercise. Many new exercise clothing materials and styles, however, work just as well.

The clothing you select for weight training should be comfortable, durable, and it should help keep your muscles warm while training. In addition you should look good and feel good about your appearance when you are weight training. If you don't feel good about yourself during an activity, the human tendency is to quit participating in the activity.

Wearing shoes when weight training is a good idea. The weight room has a number of hard objects that you might kick or drop on your feet which can injure your feet if they are not protected.

TRAINING PARTNER

A good training partner can be your greatest asset. A bad training partner can be your greatest liability. A good training partner makes training safer by being ready to spot on hazardous exercises so you can train to the limit of your capacity without fear of injury. A bad training partner is never ready when you need a spotter or is not paying attention during your exercises. A good training partner is always ready to help you load weights, change weights, and move equipment. A bad training partner lets you do all the work of setting up for exercises. A good training partner offers positive motivation and encouragement. A bad training partner maintains a negative attitude that dampens your enthusiasm. A good training partner is on time for every training session. A bad training partner frequently skips workouts or arrives late.

Even though you can make your best weight training progress with a good training partner, you can still make excellent progress training alone. A bad training partner can hinder your weight training progress. If your partner is unwilling or unable to change, you should train alone or find a new training partner. You should also be prepared to listen, as you may hear about some of your own faults as a training partner.

BASIC BARBELL GRIPS

Training with barbells, includes three basic grips: the pronated grip, the supinated grip, and the mixed grip.

- The *pronated grip* (thumbs in) also is referred to as the overhand grip, overgrip, and overgrasp, and regular grip.

- The *supinated grip* (thumbs out) also is termed the underhand grip, undergrip, undergrasp, and reverse grip.

- The *mixed grip* calls for one hand to be turned each way and also is called the combined or alternate grip.

EXERCISES

All of the exercises suggested for the beginning programs are described in the latter portion of this book. One exercise for each major muscle group or joint action is all that is needed for the beginning weight trainer. In fact, during the first year or two of training, one exercise per body part will produce good results.

Those who are weight training to develop physical fitness usually do not need to ever go beyond one exercise per body part, though occasionally changing the exercise for each body part is recommended.

More is not always better. More people have gained more muscle on simple exercise programs than all of the complicated programs combined. The following are two beginning weight training programs:

Barbell	Machine
Squat	Leg Press
Calf Raise	Calf Press
Sit-ups	Sit-ups
Dead Lift	Back Extension
Bench Press	Chest Press
BB Rowing	Rowing
Overhead Press	Overhead Press
Pull-ups	Lat Pull
Triceps Extension	Triceps Press
Barbell Curl	Arm Curl

FREQUENCY

These exercises should be performed three times each week with at least 48 hours of rest between training sessions.

SETS, REPETITIONS, AND RESISTANCE

Start Light and Progress Slowly

A person starting a weight training program should begin with light weight and progress gradually as the body adapts to the new demands being placed upon it. Weight training is one of the most intense forms of exercise available, so a muscle or group of muscles can be isolated and worked to the point of failure within a minute or two without experiencing total body fatigue. Few other training methods allow you to do that. Therefore, the beginner tends to overtrain. This tendency is also a product of the attitude, "If a little is good, more must be better." This is not always the case with physical training.

With weight training, beginners can easily overtrain the muscles to the point that they cannot recover before the next training session. The end result is either a decrease in performance or no gain. The programs suggested in this chapter are for healthy young adults of high school or college age (15 to 22 years old) who are near their peak of physical growth and who have been physically active. If you are older or have been inactive for a long time, progress should be slower.

The First Few Weeks

What is most important during the first few weeks of a weight training program? Light weights and correct exercise technique. You should learn the breathing pattern that works best and develop the habit of breathing during your exercises so that later, as the weight becomes heavier, you will not be tempted to hold your breath as you attempt to lift a difficult weight. The body should be allowed to gradually adapt to this new demand. Progress should be slow to keep muscle soreness to a minimum. You should gradually learn to increase your concentration and intensity.

Weeks One and Two (1 × 20)

For the first two weeks, each exercise should be performed once (one set), completing 20 exercise movements (20 repetitions) in that set (1 × 20). If 20 repetitions are completed with a certain amount of weight, the weight should be increased for the next training session.

Proper exercise form should not be sacrificed to complete the repetitions. When you cannot perform the repetitions in strict exercise form during a set, it is time to end that set and record the number of repetitions performed correctly.

If a weight feels very light and the repetitions are very easy, a large increase in the weight should be made for the next training session. If a weight feels moderately difficult, a small increase should be made for the next set. At the end of two weeks (six training sessions), you should be working with a weight that makes it difficult to complete 20 repetitions.

Weeks Three and Four (1 × 20) (1 × 10)

During the next two weeks (six training sessions), one set of 20 repetitions should be done as a warm-up set, and one set of 10 repetitions with a heavier weight. Each time 10 repetitions have been completed in the second set, the weight used in that set should be raised for the next training session. Following this procedure, you should be able to find the heaviest weight that you can lift 10 times while maintaining strict exercise form.

Weeks Five and Six (1 × 10) (1 × 5)

During weeks five and six (the next six workouts) one set of 10 repetitions should be performed as a warm-up set, and one set of 5 repetitions as the heavier strength development set. When you can perform 5 strict repetitions with a weight, the amount of weight used in that set should be increased for the next training session. If you cannot get at least 3 good repetitions with the new weight, however, it is too heavy and you should drop back down to your previous weight for a couple more workouts.

After the first six weeks, you should have had time to develop some basic strength and to finish reading this book so that you are able to develop your own training programs based upon the goals you have set for yourself. You also should be able to develop a method of record keeping and measuring your progress toward your goals.

SUGGESTED LIFETIME WEIGHT TRAINING PROGRAMS

The following are training programs appropriate for and popular with adults as lifetime weight training programs

(1 × 15-20)
(1 × 8-12)
(2 × 10)
(3 × 10)
(3 × 8)
(3 × 10,8,6)
(DeLorme 3 × 10)

The 1 × 15-20 workout is one in which you perform one set of each exercise, attempting to complete 20 repetitions. If you complete all 20 repetitions in good exercise form, the weight on that exercise can be increased for the next training session. You should always be able to complete at least 15 good repetitions. If you cannot complete at least 15 repetitions, the weight is too heavy. If you can complete more than 20 repetitions, the weight is too light.

The 1 × 8-12 workout is the same as the previous workout except that you should be able to get at least 8 repetitions and you should raise the weight if you can get more than 12 good strict repetitions. This and the previous workout are two fast weight training programs for those who do not want to spend much time weight training.

The 2 × 10, 3 × 10, 3 × 8 workouts can be performed using the same weight for two or three sets with a short one- or two-minute rest between sets. If you are able to complete all of the repetitions in every set, the weight can be increased for the next training session.

The 3 × 10,8,6 workout consists of three sets. The first set calls for 10 repetitions, the second set, 8 repetitions. In the third set you perform 6 repetitions. Each set is done with a heavier weight.

The DeLorme 3 × 10 workout consists of three sets of 10 repetitions:

1st set:	10 reps with	50% of 10 RM
2nd set:	10 reps with	75% of 10 RM
3rd set:	10 reps with	100% of 10 RM

The first set of 10 repetitions should be performed with 50% of your 10 repetition maximum (10-RM). Your 10-repetition maximum is the heaviest weight you can lift 10 times. The second set of 10 repetitions should be performed with 75% of your 10-repetition maximum. The third set should be performed with 100% of your 10-repetition maximum or the heaviest weight you can lift 10 times.

When you can complete 10 repetitions in the third set, the weight used in that set is raised for the next training session and the first two sets are adjusted according to this new 10-RM. You should be able to get about 8 repetitions in the last set with the new weight. Keep working with that weight until you can get 10 good repetitions. Then the weight is raised again. You should never get fewer than 6 good repetitions in the last set. If you cannot get at least 6 good repetitions, you have increased the weight too much and should reduce the weight for the next training session.

The DeLorme method is fast and easy on weight-stack machines but involves quite a bit of weight changing when using barbells, especially when alternating sets with a training partner.

7

A Formula for Success

WHAT IS SUCCESS?

"Success" has a different meaning for each of us. In presenting the formula in this chapter, success will be defined as *setting a goal and achieving it*. Successful people achieve the goals they have set for themselves. A successful person reaches big success as a result of many smaller successes. Success breeds success. Achieving smaller goals that lead to larger ones is important. This process should result in a lifestyle that is as enjoyable as the attainment of each goal.

GOALS

Goals are an extremely important part of any successful weight training program. Putting the necessary effort into weight training would be difficult without some desirable goal to be reached. In addition to the motivation factor, a successful weight training program cannot be planned without a goal. All successful training programs are based on a desired outcome. If you don't have a desired outcome, how can you plan to reach it?

Goals should be as specific as possible. This may be difficult if you are just beginning a new activity such as weight training, but try to be as specific as possible. An example of a long-term goal for a young man might be to bench press 250 pounds. For a young woman a long-term goal might be to reduce her waist circumference to 24 inches. A short-term goal for the same young man might be to increase his bench press by 10 pounds in the next three months. A short-term goal for the young woman might be to reduce her waist measurement one inch in the next two months.

Once you decide upon a goal, you should write it down. This is an important step. It is like making a contract with yourself. Your thoughts or spoken words tend to become modified with the passing of time, but your written goal will remain the same every time you read it. Once you have written your goal, you may begin to steer a course rather than to drift aimlessly. Knowing where you want to go before and during your entire journey is important.

After you have a clearly defined written goal, you will find that making decisions is easier. If you know exactly where you want to go, it is a matter of deciding, "Yes, this will take me in the right direction," or "No, this will take me in the wrong direction."

To obtain great success or achievement, goals must take into consideration your unique individual qualities. Don't set yourself up for failure. For example, most men will never bench press 600 pounds and most women will never weigh a healthy 90 pounds. Goals should be challenging, but attainable, based upon where you are starting and what you believe is possible for you.

Humans are goal-striving beings who find happiness in striving for and attaining worthwhile goals. Boredom is usually a result of not having goals. Some say that weight training is boring or that life is boring, but those who say this are probably not working toward worthwhile goals they have set for themselves. If you know what you are trying to accomplish, weight training and life become exciting adventures — not easy, but certainly not boring. When people stop striving for goals, they stop growing.

POSITIVE THINKING

Positive thinking is such an essential ingredient in success that some people have identified it as the *only* one. One reason for this is that the goal setting stage is primarily an internal process that others do not see. Positive thinking, by contrast, is obvious to everyone who comes in contact with the individual.

Your subconscious mind works on what you feed it. One sure way to short-circuit your success is to set a goal and not believe you can make it. Instead, you should fill your mind with positive thoughts, send out positive thoughts, and resist the negative thoughts of others. Positive people see the good side of bad situations and the bright side of every situation. Is a half glass of water half full or half empty? Your answer to that simple question may reveal a lot about your attitude. Many people dwell upon what they don't have and can't do; others focus upon what they do have and can do.

People should not strive for success without happiness. It would be an empty success even if the goal is achieved. Truly successful people enjoy what they are doing. Most people are as happy as they decide to be. Happiness is based on your internal reaction to external events.

Imagination is a stronger force than willpower. Form a clear, detailed image of what you really want. Everything starts with an idea. You become that which you think about. If you dwell on failure, you will fail. If you dwell on success, you will succeed. Positive thoughts create positive things.

Desire is the power behind human action. Successful people have an all-consuming, burning desire to reach their goals.

Positive thinking includes belief. Belief is more than wishing; it is knowing that you can achieve your goal.

THE SUBCONSCIOUS MIND

Nobody knows much about the subconscious mind, but we do know that it is extremely powerful and that it can help solve our problems. The subconscious mind works day and night to bring about what you imagine or visualize. That is why positive thinking is so important. If you think failure, it will help you fail. If you think success, it will help you succeed.

Your subconscious mind can be programmed through repetition. Repetition can accomplish great tasks. Therefore, you should read your goal out loud at least twice each day, morning and night, and read your weight training goal before each training session so you know why you are there and what you need to accomplish.

Humans have an opportunity to participate in their own creation. You can become what you want to become. You can be the person you want to be. To use your subconscious mind, use auto suggestion and repeat your desire or goal to yourself regularly. Once the idea is deeply embedded, the subconscious mind will go to work to help you achieve your goal. After the subconscious mind has been programmed, you need not concern yourself with how you will reach your goal; the way will appear. Keep a notepad and pencil handy for ideas; solutions will come to you. Write down these ideas immediately so you can expand on them later. Often, if they are not written down, they are gone. You may remember that you had a great idea but not be able to remember what it was.

PLANNING

Everyone has the same amount of time each week. Why do some people accomplish more than others? They learn to manage themselves and use their time wisely. Lack of time indicates lack of organization. Some people say they don't have time to exercise. What they should say is that exercise is less important to them than anything else they do.

Effectiveness means doing the right things. This requires a focus on *results*. Your time should be spent on the things that make a difference. In your weight training program, be sure you are doing the things that lead to achievement of your goal and do not waste your time on things that don't matter.

Efficiency means doing things right. This requires a focus on *methods*. Once you are doing the right exercises and you are doing the exercises right, you will be well on your way to reaching your goals.

Time should be planned to continue learning about weight training. The more you learn the better you can plan to reach your goals.

Take time to plan how you will reach your goals and continue to evaluate your progress toward your goals. After an evaluation, make the necessary adjustments in your plan.

TAKING ACTION

All of the previous steps are useless unless you take action. The world is controlled by people of action. You can never get anywhere unless you move. Therefore, decide what activities will lead to your goals, then act upon your decision. Learn to act and make things happen instead of merely reacting to things that happen to you.

Work and sacrifice are required to reach your goals. There is always a price to pay for anything that is worthwhile. You should not expect to get something for nothing. You must work at success. Once you have decided what must be done, discipline yourself to do it.

One of the most common reasons for failure is failure to take action. Procrastination probably has caused more failure than any other single factor. Now is the time to take action, not later, tomorrow, someday, or sometime. The clock is already running, and it cannot be stopped or reversed.

Once you get started, you must persist. Persistence is a familiar word but a rare quality. Many who take the first step fail because they do not continue working toward their goals. Stick with it, don't give up, never give up. If your goal is worthwhile, it is worth your best effort.

The steps in the formula for success are:

- *Define your goals.*

    Set short-term goals that you can achieve that will lead to your long-term goals.

    Fix in your mind exact measurable goals.

    Write down your goals.

- *Use positive thinking.*

    Believe you can reach your goals.

    Have faith in your ability to achieve your goals.

- *Use your subconscious mind.*

    Read your goals out loud at least twice each day, morning and night.

    Read your weight training goals before each training session.

- *Plan.*

    Take time to plan so that your efforts are directed toward your goals.

    Evaluate your progress and modify your plan.

- *Do it.*

    Start working toward your goal, and don't stop until you reach it.

    Enjoy the journey as much as the arrival.

This formula for success will work for almost anything you want. It is presented in this book to help you reach your weight training goals.

WEIGHT TRAINING GOALS

Your goals must be believable, achievable, reasonable, and attainable. Do not set yourself up for failure. A goal to bench press 1,000 pounds by the end of this year is not reasonable. A goal to lose 20 pounds of fat by the end of the week is not possible. People should set goals that they can sincerely believe in. Once you reach a goal, you can always set a higher goal. Success breeds success.

Goals must be compatible. Running the marathon in less than two hours and performing squats with 800 pounds are not compatible training goals.

Your weight training goals should be specific and measurable. Set a specific time for their attainment.

EXAMPLES OF POOR AND GOOD GOALS

Poor	Good
Increase my bench press. (no set amount, no time limit)	I will bench press 240 pounds by (specific day, month, and year.)
Firm up my muscles. (too general)	I will have a 28-inch waist by (specific day, month, year.)

If you have too many goals, a conflict of interest will almost always interfere with your progress. Rather than setting too many goals at one time, focus on a few things that are most important to you. If, however, you have several short-term body measurement goals that are compatible, and that lead to the same long-term goal of looking good, you will be all right. The goals you set must be your own, not someone else's. They must be your goals and something you want.

If you do not want to increase your muscular strength, muscular size, or muscular endurance; if you do not want to perform better, look better, or feel better; if you cannot think of any goal that weight training can help you achieve — you will probably perceive weight training to be difficult, time-consuming, and boring. If you want to increase your muscular strength, muscular size, or muscular endurance; if you want to perform better, look better, or feel better; if you can think of a goal that weight training can help you achieve — you will probably perceive weight training to be worthwhile and interesting.

8

Record Keeping and Progress

RECORD KEEPING

After setting your goals, it is important to keep track of your progress toward those goals by recording each training session. Write down what you do during each workout as soon as you have done it.

Weight training is not an exact science. Although some general guidelines have evolved for weight training, many variables affect your progress, and these can be changed. Every individual is different and therefore responds differently to a weight training stimulus. The information you record during your training sessions can be a valuable source of information about your personal response to a variety of weight training programs. You will be able to look back through your records and compare your progress with your training methods. This should help you find which exercises and training methods work best for you.

The important things to record are:

- The name of each exercise.
- The order in which exercises were performed.
- The resistance used in each set.
- The repetitions completed in each set.
- The day of the week.
- The date.

- Perhaps a general comment about how you felt or anything that might have influenced your training that day, positive or negative (for example, "felt tired, two hours sleep").

Keeping track of your weight training sessions helps to provide motivation and to ensure the correct exercise stimulus. From the written record of what you were able to do during the previous training session comes a challenge to do a little bit more — one more repetition or five more pounds. Figures 8.1 and 8.2 provide examples of written record keeping, the first informal and the second an easy-to-use form.

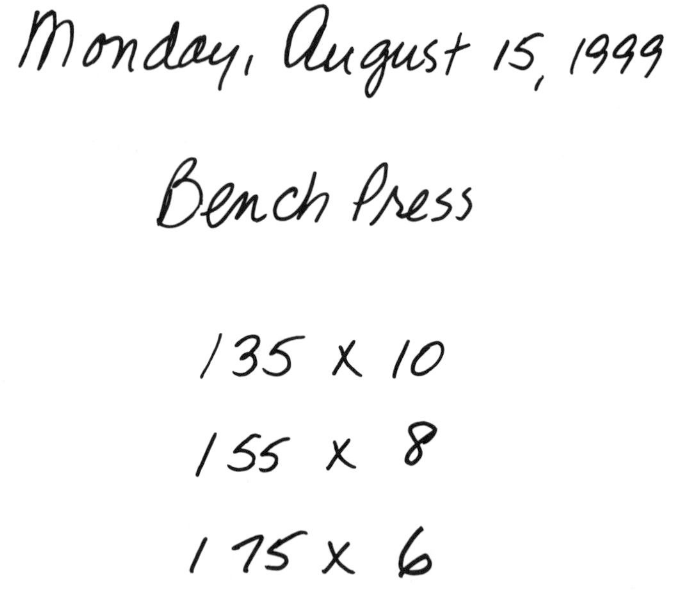

Monday, August 15, 1999

Bench Press

135 X 10

155 X 8

175 X 6

Figure 8.1 Open-Page Log

STRENGTH AND MUSCULAR ENDURANCE PROGRESS LOG

Name: _____

Day/Date	M 8/15/99															
Exercise	Wt	Rep	Wt	Rep	Wt	Rep	Wt	Rep	Wt	Rep	Wt	Rep	Wt	Rep	Wt	Rep
B Press	135	10														
	155	8														
	175	6														

Figure 8.2. Sample form for record keeping.

MEASURING PROGRESS

Measuring Strength

Strength is the ability of a muscle to exert force. If you are training with weights to gain strength, you can measure your progress by periodically testing your one-repetition maximum (1-RM) using the exercises you perform in your training program.

Your one repetition maximum is the heaviest weight you can lift one time while maintaining correct exercise technique. Of course, you will be limited to the heaviest weight you can lift through the weakest point in the range of motion. But, you will still find the heaviest weight you can lift one time, and this is a measurement of your ability to exert force (strength).

The first time you test your 1-RM, start with a light weight and perform 10 repetitions to warm up. Then add 5, 10, or 20 pounds to each subsequent set, and perform one repetition in each set until you find the heaviest weight you can lift correctly one time. Try to find your 1-RM within five or six sets. To find your maximum strength, you need to perform enough sets for the muscles to be warmed up but not so many that the muscles are fatiqued.

To perform 1-RM strength tests after the first time, start with a warm-up set of 10 repetitions with 60% of your previous 1-RM. Then perform one repetition each at 80%, 85%, 90%, and 95% of your previous 1-RM. After these progressively heavier sets, try for a new personal record based upon how the 95% load felt. If the 95% felt easy, you may want to try 10 pounds more than your previous 1-RM. If the 95% set was very hard, you may want to try just 2½ pounds or 5 pounds more than your previous 1-RM. Rest about two minutes between each set, and three to five minutes before attempting your new personal record.

If you cheat (fail to maintain correct exercise form) on a strength test in order to lift a heavier weight, you are lying to yourself about your true strength level. You also have a greater risk of injury when you begin to perform exercises improperly to lift a greater weight than you can really handle.

Always use spotters for the exercises in which you could get trapped under a heavy weight. Do not try to perform 1-RMs in all of your exercises.

As a beginning weight trainer you might want to test 1-RMs once a month for the first six to 12 months. After that, increases come more slowly, so testing once every two or three months might be adequate.

Measuring Muscular Endurance

Muscular endurance is the ability of a muscle to exert force for a long time or for many repetitions. If you are training with weights to gain muscular endurance, you can measure your progress by performing as many consecutive repetitions as possible with an established weight.

Select a weight that is at least 50% but not more than 70% of your one-repetition maximum. Perform as many continuous repetitions as possible without any pause between repetitions. Maintain strict exercise form.

Repeat this test once a month using the same weight every time. An increase in the number of repetitions you can complete is evidence of an increase in your muscle endurance.

Measuring Size

The most common way to measure changes in muscle size is to measure the circumference of various body parts with a tape measure. Although circumference measurements include many other kinds of tissue (bone, fat, blood vessels, skin, and so on), muscle and fat are the two tissues that change the most. If you are training your muscles hard and eating properly, circumference gains should be a result of increased muscle and losses should be a result of decreased fat.

Have your training partner measure you. A Gulick tape measure is ideal if one is available. A Gulick tape has a spring tension device on the end so that all measurements may be made with the same tension on the tape. If a Gulick tape is not available and measurements are taken with a standard cloth tape measure, the tape should be placed around the circumference so that it is firm but not so tight that the skin is indented. Measure to the nearest eighth of an inch or half centimeter.

Measurements commonly taken by men and women who wish to change their appearance are listed here. These represent the circumference measurements that are most likely to change in response to a weight training program. For some body parts two measurements are described, relaxed and flexed. If you are trying to lose excess body fat, use the relaxed measurements. If you are trying to gain muscle size, use the flexed measurements. The measurements should be taken while you are in a standing position with your feet about six inches apart. The tape measure should be horizontal unless the directions for a body part specify something different.

Neck   *Relaxed*: Measure the horizontal circumference midway between the shoulders and the head.

Shoulders   *Relaxed*: Measure horizontal circumference of the body at the level of greatest shoulder width with both arms hanging relaxed.

Chest   *Relaxed*: Measure at the largest circumference during relaxed breathing. Do not lift your chest or flex your muscles.

                    Flexed (Expanded): Measure at the largest circumference of the chest with the lungs filled, rib cage lifted, and muscles flexed.

Waist   *Relaxed*: Measure the horizontal circumference at the level of the navel. The abdominal muscles should be in their normal state of tonus for a relaxed standing position.

                    Flexed: Measure the horizontal circumference with the abdomen pulled in as far as possible.

Hips   *Relaxed*: Measure at the largest horizontal circumference.

                    Flexed: Tighten the muscles in the hip region and measure at the largest horizontal circumference.

For all of the following arm and leg measurements, the tape should be held perpendicular to the limb segment being measured. Measure both arms and both legs.

Thigh   *Relaxed*: Measure the horizontal circumference midway between the hip joint and the knee joint.

                    Flexed: Slightly bend the knee joint and contract all of the thigh muscles. Measure midway between the hip joint and the knee joint.

Calf or Leg   *Relaxed*: Measure at the largest circumference.

Flexed: Measure the largest circumference with the muscles of the leg flexed.

Upper Arm   *Relaxed*: With the arms hanging relaxed, measure the horizontal circumference midway between the shoulder joint and the elbow joint.

Flexed: Raise your arm to shoulder height and to the side of your body. Bend your elbow and flex all of the muscles of the upper arm. Measure the largest circumference.

Forearm   *Relaxed*: With both arms hanging in a normal relaxed position, measure the largest circumference of the forearm, between the wrist and the elbow.

Flexed: Bend your elbow and wrist so that as many forearm muscles as possible can be contracted. Measure at the largest circumference between the wrist and the elbow.

All of these measurements should be taken the first time you are measured. After that you may choose to measure just the ones you are the most interested in. Beginning weight trainers might want to measure once a month for the first year. After the first year, changes tend to come more slowly so you might want to take measurements once every two or three months.

No standard set of body circumference measurements is available. The ones suggested here are those that are commonly used. Because they are used to measure your progress, muscle gain or fat loss, they should be taken exactly the same way each time and, if possible, with the same tape measure. Remember that these measurements are to provide information about the effectiveness of your training program.

Measuring Body Weight

If your goal is to change your body weight, this can be measured easily on an accurate scale. It is best to use the same scale, at the same time of day, wearing as little clothing as possible, and the same clothing each time.

Measuring Body Fat

Skinfold measurements should be taken at the sites where you are most interested in losing excess body fat. There are standard measurement procedures for the different sites. These measurements should be taken by someone who is trained and experienced.

Changes in Appearance

Changes that take place in appearance are gradual and cannot be seen as they occur. Photographs of various poses can be an excellent means for periodically checking your progress. A photograph is the only way to really see yourself. Obviously the photograph should be taken while you are wearing as little clothing as possible, such as a swimsuit. Subsequent photographs should be taken with the same camera, location, position, and distance.

When training to improve appearance, many men are interested in developing muscle size. Muscle size, however, should not be increased without regard to balance and symmetry. Some men have trained one body part until it does not look like it belongs on their body. This does not present an attractive or appealing appearance.

PROGRESS EVALUATION

Progress should not be checked too often. Physical changes take time. Beginners might be able to measure once a month and see progress, but more advanced weight trainers might only check once or twice a year.

GENETIC POTENTIAL

Each individual has some upper limit on the amount of strength or size he or she can gain. For the beginning weight trainer, gains are relatively easy and fast. As progress continues and gains get close to a person's genetic limit, the gains become more difficult and slower.

One of the most intriguing aspects of weight training is that you have no way of knowing when you have reached your genetic limit, or in fact if anyone has ever reached their limit. After years of weight training, body builders and strength athletes continue to improve, though the rate of improvement slows down.

PROBLEM SOLVING

When you are not making progress toward your goal for a long time, (two or three months), problem solving is in order. What might be responsible for your lack of progress? Change the one thing that you think is the most likely cause of your lack of progress. Allow three or four weeks for the change to start making a difference. After a month if no progress occurs, try changing a different variable. Give it time to work.

Changing more than one variable at a time may leave you with more questions than answers. Changing too often (less than four to six weeks) does not allow enough time to find out what works for you and what does not. Keep in mind that what works for you now may not work when your body adapts to it.

Some of the factors to consider in solving your lack of progress in weight training are:

amount of resistance
number of repetitions
number of sets
rest between sets
number of exercises per body part
total number of exercises performed
order of exercises
frequency of training
concentration during exercise performance
intensity of training
regularity of training, hour and day
motivation level
nutrition
rest
other activities
mental stress
drugs
alcohol
tobacco

9

Planning a Weight Training Program

BASIC WEIGHT TRAINING PRINCIPLES

There are three basic principles behind all weight training progress. They are specificity, overload, and progression.

Specificity

You must exercise the specific muscles that you want to develop. You must also follow specific exercise guidelines to produce the specific type of change you want to occur: muscle strength, muscle size, muscle endurance, or muscle tone.

Overload

The overload principle is the basis of all training programs. In weight training that means the muscle to be developed must be overloaded, or forced to work harder than normal.

Progression

Once your muscles adjust to a given workload, it is no longer an overload. The work load must be gradually increased as the muscle adapts to each new demand.

CONSIDERATIONS IN PLANNING YOUR WEIGHT TRAINING PROGRAM

Your Goals

Planning a weight training program must begin with what you wish to accomplish. You can train for three basic aspects of muscle fitness:

- Muscle strength.
- Muscle size.
- Muscle endurance.

Any weight training program you choose will result in some increase in all three areas. Untrained beginners gain on almost any weight training program as long as progressive overload is applied. Some general guidelines have emerged from research and experience, however, that will help you focus on developing the aspect you are most interested in.

Which Exercises

Among the many weight training exercises to choose from, which ones are the best? The best weight training exercises are compound exercises, which require more than one joint or muscle to move the weight. With compound exercises, such as the squat and the bench press, large amounts of muscle are exercised at the same time. Exercises that require both arms or both legs to work together allow the use of more weight and maintain a balance of development on both sides of the body.

Almost all weight trainers use the same basic exercises. These exercises are included in the beginner or basic weight training program in this book.

Choose exercises for your training program with overall development in mind. Developing the entire body is better than ignoring certain body parts or over-developing one or two body parts. As you select your exercises, keep balanced development in mind. Both sides of the body should be developed equally, and the opposing muscle or muscle group should always be exercised. In the beginning, if you do not know the muscles, remember that for every exercise action or movement you perform, there should be an opposite action or movement in another exercise. For example, if you perform an exercise that develops elbow flexion, you should also do an exercise that develops elbow extension.

Isolation exercises with dumbbells are used primarily by body builders in the final preparation for a contest.

Number of Exercises

One exercise per body part is enough for the beginning weight trainer. In fact, one exercise per body part is enough for all but the most advanced high-level strength athletes and body builders. For the first year or two of training, more than one exercise for each muscle group may result in overtraining and slow your progress. One exercise for each major muscle group or body part will result in about 8 to 12 basic exercises in your training program.

Order of Exercises

Exercise the largest muscles first and work your way down to the smallest muscles last. The largest muscles require the most energy and need the smaller muscles to assist. If the smaller muscles are already fatigued, you will have difficulty handling enough weight to properly exercise the larger muscles. For example, most back exercises require elbow flexion. If the elbow flexors have already been exercised, they will fatigue before the larger back muscles do. The largest muscles are located on the torso. Proceeding outward on the arms and legs, the muscles get smaller.

The order of exercises may also be based on a *work-rest principle*. If a muscle is worked during an exercise, it is allowed to rest during the next exercise. If you are exercising opposing muscle groups, you may work a muscle, then let it rest as you work on the opposing muscle. This allows you to complete more work in less time.

Another consideration in the order of exercises is whether to perform a circuit or to do the exercises in a traditional (non-circuit) manner. When you perform a circuit, you do each exercise in your training program once in a specified order. Then you perform each exercise again (and possibly again) in that same order. The traditional way of lifting weights is to do all of the sets of one exercise before moving to the next exercise.

Resistance

The amount of weight you use depends upon what you want to develop. The general rule is that for *strength* you need a heavy weight and few repetitions. For muscle *endurance* you need a light weight and more repetitions. Muscle *size* development is in between, calling for moderate weight and repetitions. Before the heavy weight of strength training, you should complete warm-up sets.

Strength	85% to 100% of 1-RM
Muscle size	70% to 85% of 1-RM
Muscle endurance	50% to 70% of 1-RM

Starting Weight

Begin with a weight that is light so you can easily perform each exercise correctly. The resistance should be increased gradually. Don't be in too big of a hurry to load up on resistance. If you give your body time to adapt, you will experience more progress, less muscle soreness, and less frustration. You have plenty of time to add weight if you are weight training for life.

Repetitions

The resistance you choose will affect the repetitions that you perform:

Strength	1-5 repetitions
Muscle size	6-12 repetitions
Muscle endurance	20-50 repetitions

Most experienced weight trainers do moderate to high repetitions when they exercise the abdominals, lower back, forearms, and calves.

Sets

The resistance and repetitions influence the number of sets you will be able to perform for each exercise:

Strength	4-8 sets
Muscle size	3-6 sets
Muscle Endurance	2-4 sets

Rest

The amount of rest between sets is determined by what you are trying to develop:

Strength	2-4 minutes
Muscle size	1-2 minutes
Muscle endurance	30-90 seconds

Frequency

A muscle usually requires two or three days of rest to recover and adapt before it should be exercised again. Exercising a muscle three days per week with 48 to 72 hours of rest between training sessions works well for most weight trainers. Advanced weight trainers perform different exercises on different days so they may exercise four, five, or six days a week; they do not exercise the same body parts each day.

Fixed or Variable Exercise Load

A load is applied to each exercise in two basic ways: fixed or variable. With a *fixed load* the resistance, repetitions, sets and rest interval remain the same (fixed) during a training session for an exercise.

Example:
Bench Press
150 pounds
10 repetitions
3 sets
1 minute rest between sets

With a *variable method* of loading, the resistance, repetitions, and rest interval change for each set of an exercise.

Example:
Bench Press
150 lbs 10 reps 1 min. rest
170 lbs　8 reps 2 min. rest
190 lbs　6 reps 3 min. rest
210 lbs　4 reps 4 min. rest

Progression

Some general rules will be helpful in applying the progression principle to the overload:

- Increase only one variable at a time (resistance, repetitions, sets, rest).
- Increase reps or sets before increasing resistance.
- Decrease reps when increasing resistance.
- Decrease the rest interval between sets to increase muscular endurance.

Muscle Tone or Muscle Fitness

Beginners often say they just want to tone the muscles. They are not especially interested in developing strength, size, or endurance.

What is muscle tone? When the word "tone" is used in reference to muscle tissue, it refers to muscle tissue that is firm, sound, and resilient. This is in contrast to the loose, flabby, and weak muscle tone of the sedentary person. Although the former is desirable, measuring changes in muscle tone is rather difficult.

Whether a person chooses to train for strength, size, or endurance, an improvement in muscle tone will occur. Also, if an individual chooses to train for muscle tone, some improvement will occur in strength, size, and muscle endurance. These improvements, however, will be more gradual and more difficult to measure.

Some guidelines for those who wish to train for muscle fitness or muscle tone are:

   60% to 80% of 1-RM
   8 to 12 repetitions
   1 to 3 sets of each exercise
   30 to 60 seconds rest between sets
   3 days per week (every other day)

Although training for muscle tone is possible, the lack of measurable progress can result in a loss of motivation for beginners. Therefore, beginning weight trainers are advised to work toward changes in strength, size, or muscle endurance, which can be measured more easily. Measured progress is evidence that weight training is effective, and it serves as a motivating influence to continue.

Table 9.1. Summary of Weight Training Guidelines

	Muscle Strength	Muscle Size	Muscle Endurance	Muscle Tone
Resistance	85% to 100% of 1-RM	70% to 85% of 1-RM	50% to 70% of 1-RM	60% to 80% of 1-RM
Repetitions	1 to 5	6 to 12	20 to 50	8 to 12
Sets	4 to 8	3 to 6	2 to 4	1 to 3
Rest (between sets)	2 to 4 minutes	1 to 2 minutes	30 to 90 seconds	30 to 60 seconds
Frequency	3 days per week	3 days per week	3 days per week	3 days per week

10

Advanced Weight Training

PROGRESSIVE OVERLOAD

Progressive overload is the basis of all successful weight training programs. The muscles can be overloaded in many ways. The overload that the muscles experience depends upon all of the following variables:

- Which exercises are performed.
- How many total exercises are performed.
- How many exercises are performed for each body part.
- Order in which exercises are performed.
- Amount of resistance or weight used in each set.
- Number of repetitions per set.
- Number of sets per exercise.
- Amount of rest between sets.
- Frequency of training sessions.
- Method of progression.
- Whether the exercise load is fixed or variable.
- Whether the total body is exercised in each training session or is divided into a split routine.
- Exercise intensity.

These variables may be changed and combined in a seemingly unlimited number of ways. Some of the more common training programs will be presented to give you an idea of the variety available to you in weight training. All of these training programs are different ways to arrive at the same thing: progressive overload.

Beginning weight trainers tend to gain on almost any weight training program. The greatest danger for beginners is over-training. If you find yourself training very hard, not making any progress, and feeling tired all the time, you are probably overtraining and should try less exercise and more rest.

Humans cannot maintain absolute peak condition for very long — probably a few weeks at best. Therefore, highly trained advanced weight trainers, competitive lifters, and body builders use periodization or cycling. They divide the year into periods or cycles, then vary their training methods and intensity during the cycles so that they reach their peak condition during their competitive season, and hopefully for their most important contest of the year.

INCREASING EXERCISE INTENSITY

One of the first things that weight trainers try to do as they advance in their training is to increase the intensity of their exercise. The following are seven common methods of increasing exercise intensity.

Concentric Failure

To reach concentric failure, you must perform repetitions until you cannot perform another repetition while maintaining strict exercise form.

Forced Reps

Forced reps are repetitions performed after reaching concentric failure. When you cannot perform another repetition correctly by yourself, a spotter assists as little as possible to help you complete one or two more repetitions.

Negatives

You can lower a heavier weight than you can lift. Negatives are performed by having spotters help you lift a weight and then allowing you to lower the weight by yourself. This is an advanced training method that can result in extreme muscle soreness. It is not recommended for beginning weight trainers.

Eccentric Failure

When you perform negatives (lower a weight) until you can no longer control the speed at which you lower the weight, you have reached eccentric failure. This is obviously dangerous and is not recommended for beginners.

Cheating

Cheating is the use of body movement to get past the weakest point in the range of motion of an exercise. It can be a useful means for advanced lifters to add to the overload; however, most weight trainers cheat to make the exercise easier.

Pre-Exhaustion

Pre-exhaustion involves performing an isolation exercise for a muscle and following this immediately by a compound exercise. The idea is to work the muscle to concentric failure with the isolation exercise, then to force the muscle to continue working with the assistance of other muscles that are not exhausted.

Cycle or Periodization

Advanced lifters use training cycles or periods in which they progressively increase exercise intensity to reach a peak during their competitive season. Beginning weight trainers do not need to use any of these methods of increasing exercise intensity as long as steady progress is occurring. Most of these techniques are used only for a short period by advanced weight trainers to overcome a plateau, or period of no improvement.

TOTAL BODY AND SPLIT ROUTINES

Total Body Training Routines

Beginners and fitness weight trainers usually perform all of their weight training exercises at one time and repeat this procedure every other day. They exercise the total body in one training session.

Split Routines

As weight trainers advance and the total work load increases, many choose to split their exercises, performing part of them one day and the rest of them on another day. One example is the four-day split, in which half of the exercises are performed on Monday and Thursday and the other half on Tuesday and Friday. An example of a four-day split is a push-pull routine in which the pushing exercises are performed on Monday and Thursday and the pulling exercises on Tuesday and Friday.

Most advanced body builders go to a six-day split as they near competition. In a six-day split they perform about a third of their exercises on Monday and Thursday, a third on Tuesday and Friday, and a third on Wednesday and Saturday. The ultimate split is the blitz routine, in which they exercise only one body part each day.

FIXED SYSTEMS

Fixed systems are those in which variables are not changed during a training session but a variable may be changed for the next training session.

Simple Progressive System

A simple progressive system involves changing only one variable, such as the resistance. One example would be performing one set of 10 repetitions of an exercise. If 10 repetitions were completed, the weight would be increased for the next training session.

Double Progressive System

A double progressive system calls for changing two variables, such as resistance and repetitions. One example would be performing one set of 12 repetitions. Because 12 repetitions were completed, the weight would be increased for the next training session and the repetitions would be decreased to 8. The repetitions then would be increased by one each training session until one set of 12 repetitions is completed with the new weight. Then the weight would be increased and the repetitions decreased again. This pattern continues — increasing the repetitions, then the weight.

One Set to Failure

A variation of the double progressive system is one set to failure. In this system one set of each exercise is performed to the point at which you cannot perform another repetition and still maintain correct exercise form. A weight is used that causes this failure to occur between 8 and 12 repetitions. When you complete 12 repetitions, the weight is raised for the next training session.

Set System

The set system requires performing more than one set of each exercise. In a fixed system the repetitions remain the same for each set. One example is three sets of six repetitions. When you can perform six repetitions in all three sets, the weight is raised for the next training session. This is a good program if you are training with barbells because it reduces the amount of time you spend changing weights.

Circuit System

A series of exercises is performed in a sequence or circuit with one exercise at each station. You move from one exercise to the next, performing one set of each exercise until you have completed every exercise in the circuit once. The entire circuit then may be repeated. A circuit usually is completed one to three times during a training session.

Circuit training often is used with a large group when time and equipment are limited. This is often the case with athletic teams. Circuit training allows a large number of people to get a good workout in a short time.

Aerobic Circuit System

In an aerobic weight training circuit, exercises are performed one right after the other with very little rest between exercises. This is done to keep the heart rate elevated during the entire circuit and thus produce a training effect for the cardiovascular system.

Super Set System

A super set requires performing two exercises in a sequence, followed by a rest interval. Often, opposing muscle groups are exercised in this manner. For example, the first set might consist of barbell curls for the elbow flexors. The next exercise could be tricep extensions for the elbow extensors. Because these muscles work in opposition to one another, one of them is resting while the other is working. After one set of each exercise, there is usually a rest interval before repeating the sequence. This is a good way to reduce training time without reducing the amount of work completed during the training session. It is like a mini-circuit.

Giant Sets

Giant sets usually involve three to five exercises for the same muscle. One set of each exercise is performed with little or no rest between sets. After all of the exercises in the sequence have been performed, there is a rest interval before the sequence is repeated. This is a highly advanced training system that some body builders use.

Rest-Pause System

The rest-pause system has many variations. Here is one: Perform an exercise to the point of temporary muscular failure, hold the weight while the muscle recovers slightly, perform another repetition, pause, do another repetition, continue until no more repetitions can be performed.

VARIABLE SYSTEMS

In variable systems one or more variables are altered during the performance of one exercise.

Pyramid System

In a pyramid system the weight used for each set of an exercise is increased and the number of repetitions is decreased correspondingly. This allows the exerciser to proceed from a light weight to a heavy weight. This system is used most often by those training for strength. Some choose to pyramid up only; others pyramid up to a heavy weight, then back down again.

Percentage System

This is a variation of the pyramid system. Multiple sets of an exercise are performed at various percentages of the one-repetition maximum for that exercise. The percentages usually start out low in the first set and increase in each of the subsequent sets.

DeLorme System

One good percentage system for beginners, and those training for fitness, is the DeLorme system.

1st set	10 reps	50% of 10-RM
2nd set	10 reps	75% of 10-RM
3rd set	10 reps	100% of 10-RM

Continuous Set System

In the continuous set system you start with a weight that you can use to complete a given number of repetitions — for example, 10 repetitions. When you reach the point at which you can do no more repetitions, your training partners quickly remove a small amount of weight while you continue to hold the bar or stay in position on the machine. As soon as some weight has been removed, the exercise is continued until you cannot do any more repetitions. Once again, your training partners remove a small amount of weight. This process continues until you cannot do any more repetitions, even with the lightest weight.

Light to Heavy System

In this variation of the pyramid and continuous set systems, you start with a light to moderate weight and perform three repetitions. Your training partners quickly add a small amount of weight. After three more repetitions you again add weight. This process continues until you can perform only one repetition.

Tonnage System

The resistance and repetitions vary in the tonnage system, but the lifter keeps track of the total pounds lifted in a training session. This is used most often by competitive weight lifters.

These are only a few of the methods that advanced weight trainers have used to improve their training progress. Many more are in use.

TRAINING EQUIPMENT

Fixed Resistance Equipment

Barbells, dumbbells, and some weight-stack equipment have a resistance that is a fixed weight. The weight remains the same throughout the exercise. Because of changes in leverage at the joints involved during movement through the full range of motion, this fixed weight is more difficult to lift at some joint angles and easier at others.

With fixed resistance equipment you are limited to the heaviest weight you can lift through the weakest point in the range of motion. Two basic equipment design approaches have attempted to overcome this limitation: variable resistance equipment and isokinetic equipment.

Variable Resistance Equipment

Some weight-stack equipment has been designed so that as changes in leverage take place for the working muscles and joints, the exercise machine makes compensating leverage changes. When you are exercising with fixed resistance equipment, once you can get past the weakest point in the range of motion, the rest of the exercise movement is fairly easy. With the compensating leverage change of variable resistance equipment, the muscle must continue to work hard throughout the full range of motion.

The weight in the stack lifted remains constant, but the leverage change in the machine makes the resistance greater at some joint angles and less at other joint angles. The intent of variable resistance equipment is to keep the muscles fully loaded throughout the full range of motion.

Isokinetic Equipment

Isokinetic equipment offers another solution to keeping the muscle fully loaded throughout the full range of motion. Isokinetic refers to constant motion or constant speed. True isokinetic exercise equipment limits the speed at which the exercise device will move. Therefore, a muscle can contract at its maximum force from full extension to full contraction without producing acceleration.

Which Type of Exercise Equipment is the Best?

So far, no one particular type of exercise equipment has been proven superior for the development of muscle tissue. Muscles don't know or care what type of exercise equipment is used to provide the resistance as long as they receive the same overload stimulus.

11

Barbell and Dumbbell Exercises

EXERCISES FOR DIFFERENT BODY PARTS

There are many barbell and dumbbell exercises, and several variations of each exercise. This chapter presents some of the more common exercises for you to try. As you progress in your weight training and plan new exercise programs, you will want to attempt new exercises to add interest and excitement to your training. The exercises in this chapter are arranged in the following order:

Chest
    Bench Press
    Incline Bench Press
    Straight-Arm Pullover
    Bent-Arm Pullover
    Cross-Bench Pullover
    Bent-Arm Flyes

Back
    Dead Lift
    Power Cleans
    Shoulder Shrug
    Barbell Rowing
    Chin-Ups

Pull-Ups
Pull-Ups Behind the Neck
One-Dumbbell Rowing

Shoulders

Military Press
Press Behind the Neck
Upright Rowing
Lateral Raise
Bent-Over Lateral Raise
Front Raise

Upper Arm (elbow flexors)

Barbell Curl
Reverse Curl
Incline Dumbbell Curl
Seated Dumbbell Curl

Upper Arm (elbow extensors)

Standing Tricep Extension
Lying Tricep Extension
Close-Grip Bench Press

Forearm

Barbell Wrist Curl
Reverse Wrist Curl

Thigh

Squat
Front Squat
Lunge
Bench Step

Leg

Standing Barbell Calf Raise
One-Dumbbell Calf Raise
Donkey Calf Raise

CONCENTRIC AND ECCENTRIC PHASES

Concentric Phase

The concentric phase of a weight training exercise is the portion of the exercise during which the muscular contractions overcome the resistance and the weight is lifted.

Eccentric Phase

The eccentric phase of a weight training exercise is the portion of the exercise during which the resistance overcomes the muscular contraction and the weight is lowered.

The same muscles are working during both the concentric phase and the eccentric phase of a weight training exercise. Do not perform half an exercise; the weight should be controlled and the muscles loaded all the way up and all the way down.

DUMBBELLS

Almost any barbell exercise also can be performed using dumbbells. Advanced body builders use dumbbells for isolation exercises. In many dumbbell exercises the dumbbells may be moved together or in an alternating manner.

CHEST EXERCISES

BENCH PRESS

Muscles developed: Pectoralis major, anterior deltoid, triceps.

Starting position: Lie on your back on a flat bench; hold a barbell directly above your shoulders, arms straight, and both feet flat on the floor.

Eccentric phase: Inhale as you lower the bar to touch your chest.

Concentric phase: Exhale as you press the weight back up to the starting position.

Spotting: Have a spotter stand at the head end of the bench just in case you get stuck with the weight on your chest.

Variations: Change the angle of the bench and change the width of the hand spacing on the bar to achieve many variations of this basic chest exercise.

Additional information: To make this exercise easier to perform, use a rack to hold the weight above the bench.

INCLINE BENCH PRESS

Muscles developed: Upper pectoralis major, anterior deltoid, tricep.

Starting position: Lie on your back on an incline bench; hold a barbell directly above your shoulders with both arms straight, and both feet flat on the floor.

Eccentric phase: Inhale as you lower the bar to touch your chest.

Concentric phase: Exhale as you press the weight back up to the starting position.

Spotting: Have a spotter stand behind the bench in case you cannot get the weight back to the starting position.

Variations:

1. Change the angle of the incline bench.
2. Change the hand spacing on the bar.

Additional Information: To make this exercise easier to perform, use a weight rack to support the weight above the bench.

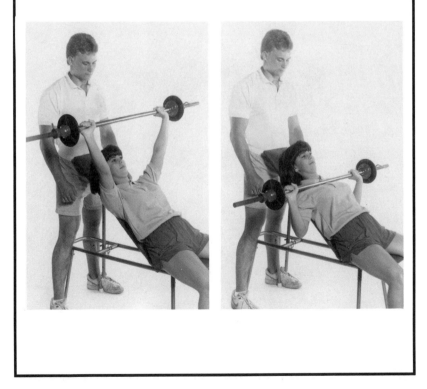

STRAIGHT-ARM PULLOVER

Muscles developed: Primarily an exercise to lift and expand the rib cage.

Starting position: Lie on your back on a flat bench; hold a barbell directly above your shoulders, with your hand spacing about shoulder width.

Eccentric phase: Inhale deeply as you lower the bar overhead, keeping your arms straight. When you reach the end of this motion, hold this fully stretched position for three to five seconds with as much air in the lungs as they will hold.

Concentric phase: Exhale as you return the bar to the starting position.

Additional information: As this is primarily a stretching exercise to lift and expand the rib cage, do not attempt to handle heavy weight in this exercise.

BENT-ARM PULLOVER

Muscles developed: Latissimus dorsi, pectoralis major.

Starting position: Lie on your back on a flat bench; hold a barbell supported on your chest, hands 6 to 12 inches apart, elbows bent, and head hanging beyond the end of the bench.

Eccentric phase: Inhale as you lower the weight past your face toward the floor.

Concentric phase: Exhale as you pull the weight from the floor to the starting position.

Additional information: Keep your elbows bent and your arms in close to your head.

CROSS-BENCH PULLOVER

Muscles developed: Primarily a stretching exercise to lift and expand the rib cage.

Starting position: Lie across an exercise bench with your shoulders on the bench; hold a dumbbell with both hands directly above your shoulders, keeping the arms straight.

Eccentric phase: Inhale as deeply as you can while lowering the weight overhead. Keep your arms straight. Hold the fully stretched position three to five seconds while maintaining as much air in your lungs as possible.

Concentric phase: Exhale as you return to the starting position.

Additional information: As this is primarily a stretching exercise to lift and expand the rib cage, do not attempt to use heavy weight in this exercise.

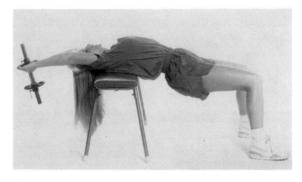

BENT-ARM FLYES

Muscles developed: Pectoralis major, anterior deltoid.

Starting position: Lie on your back on a flat exercise bench; hold one dumbbell in each hand above the shoulders, with your arms slightly bent.

Eccentric phase: Inhale as you move the dumbbells away from each other and lower them toward the floor.

Concentric phase: Exhale as you return the dumbbells to the starting position.

Variations: Perform this exercise on an incline or decline bench.

Additional information: Keep your elbows slightly bent throughout this exercise to place the exercise stress on the pectoralis major muscle and relieve the stress on the elbow joint.

BACK EXERCISES

DEAD LIFT

Muscles developed: Erector spinae, gluteus maximus, quadriceps, trapezius, rhomboids.

Starting position: Bend over and assume a mixed grip on a barbell that is lying on the floor; bend your knees and hips so that the hips are approximately knee level; keep your back flat.

Concentric phase: Keep your neck and back flat while straightening the hips and knees to arrive at a standing position.

Eccentric phase: Keep your neck and back flat as you slowly lower the weight back to the floor by bending your knees and hips.

Additional information: Extremely heavy weight can be handled in this exercise. Progress slowly, and maintain correct lifting position. Progressing too quickly or using improper lifting technique may result in injury.

POWER CLEANS

Muscles developed: Trapezius, erector spinae, gluteus maximus, quadriceps.

Starting position: Bend over and grasp a barbell that is lying on the floor, with your hands approximately shoulder-width apart and in a pronated (thumbs in) grip; bend your knees and hips so that your knees are at a 90° angle; keep your head in line with your body, with your neck and back flat.

Concentric phase: Inhale as you lift the bar from the floor and accelerate the bar upward, gaining speed as it rises to the highest position to which you can pull it. The pull should continue upward to the level of your chest or shoulders. As the bar nears its highest point, quickly rotate your arms under the bar and bend your knees, catching the bar on your shoulders. Straighten your legs to a standing position and exhale.

Eccentric phase: Inhale and quickly rotate the arms from under the bar. Bend your arms, legs, and hips to decelerate the bar to a hang position with the bar resting against the upper thighs. Then slowly bend the knees and hips to lower the bar back to the floor. Exhale.

Variations:

1. Start with the weight up on blocks.
2. Start with the weight in a hang position (hang cleans).

Additional information: Keep your back straight. Do not jerk the weight from the floor, but lift and accelerate the weight.

SHOULDER SHRUG

Muscles developed: Trapezius, levator scapulae.

Starting position: Stand with a barbell hanging at arms-length in front of your body; hold the bar with both hands in a pronated (thumbs in) grip.

Concentric phase: Inhale as you lift or shrug your shoulders to the highest possible position. Hold that position briefly.

Eccentric phase: Exhale as you slowly lower the shoulders back to the starting position.

Variations:

1. Roll the shoulders forward and up, then back and down.
2. Roll the shoulders back and up, then forward and down.

Additional information: Do not bend your elbows or pull with your arm muscles. The hands and arms serve as hooks to hang the weight on during this exercise. Do not jerk the weight upward or let it drop back to the starting position.

BARBELL ROWING

Muscles developed: Latissimus dorsi, teres major, posterior deltoid, trapezius, rhomboids.

Starting position: Bend over; with your knees slightly bent, hold a barbell in your hands with your arms straight so that the barbell is hanging directly below your shoulders.

Concentric phase: Exhale as the weight is pulled upward until the bar touches your chest.

Eccentric phase: Inhale as the weight is lowered to the starting position.

Variations:

1. Standing on a bench or block to get more stretch in the starting position as the weight increases and larger plates are used.
2. Change the distance between your hands, which results in several variations of this exercise.
3. Pull the bar to the shoulders, chest, or abdomen.
4. Perform this exercise with dumbbells, either bringing both up at the same time or alternately.

Additional information: Keep your back as flat as possible throughout this exercise. Do not jerk or drop the weight. Keep the knees slightly bent to reduce the stress on the lower back. Perform this exercise with caution and common sense. The lower back is in a potentially dangerous position. To make this exercise safer for the lower back, perform it with your forehead supported on a solid object that is about waist high.

CHIN-UPS

Muscles developed: Latissimus dorsi, teres major, biceps brachii.

Starting position: Hang from a chinning bar with a supinated (thumbs out) grip.

Concentric phase: Exhale as you pull yourself upward to a position with your chin above the bar.

Eccentric phase: Inhale as you slowly lower yourself to the starting position.

Variations: Change grip spacing for several good variations of this exercise.

Additional information: Start each chin-up from a full hang. Do not bounce, kick, or use a whipping motion of the body, because that will reduce the effectiveness of the exercise. One of the best ways to add weight to this exercise is to hang a dumbbell from a wide strap that passes behind your lower back and place the dumbbell between your thighs to keep it from swinging.

PULL-UPS

Muscles developed: Latissimus dorsi, teres major, biceps brachii.

Starting position: Hang from a bar with a pronated (thumbs in) grip.

Concentric phase: Exhale as you pull yourself upward to a position with your chin above the bar.

Eccentric phase: Inhale as you slowly lower yourself to the starting position.

Variations: Change grip spacing for several good variations of this exercise.

Additional information: Start each pull-up from a full hang. Pause with your chin above the bar, and slowly lower yourself to the starting position. Add weight by suspending a dumbbell from a wide strap that passes around the lower back and placing the dumbbell between the thighs.

PULL-UPS BEHIND THE NECK

Muscles developed: Latissimus dorsi, teres major, biceps brachii.

Starting position: Hang from a bar with a wide pronated (thumbs in) grip.

Concentric phase: Exhale as you pull yourself upward to a position where your upper back touches the bar.

Eccentric phase: Inhale as you slowly lower yourself to the starting position.

Variations: With the same hand spacing, pull upward with the bar passing in front of your face until your chest touches the bar.

Additional information: Start from a fully stretched hang position. Pause briefly at the top. Lower slowly to the starting position. Add weight by placing a dumbbell, suspended by a wide strap around the lower back, between the thighs.

ONE-DUMBBELL ROWING

Muscles developed: Latissimus dorsi, teres major, rhomboids, trapezius.

Starting position: Place one hand and the same-side knee on an exercise bench, the foot of the opposite leg on the floor, and the hand on that side of the body holding a dumbbell hanging at arms-length below the shoulder.

Concentric phase: Exhale as you pull the dumbbell upward until it touches your chest.

Eccentric phase: Inhale as you slowly lower the dumbbell to the starting position.

Variations: Bring the dumbbell to the shoulder or waist.

Additional information: Use the hand and forearm as a hook to the hold the weight while the back muscles pull the elbow to its highest position.

SHOULDER EXERCISES

MILITARY PRESS

Muscles developed: Deltoid, triceps.

Starting position: Stand with a barbell supported at shoulder level in front of your body, your hands placed slightly wider apart than shoulder-width.

Concentric phase: Inhale while pressing the weight overhead to a straight-arm position.

Eccentric phase: Exhale while lowering the weight to the starting position.

Variations: Sit on a flat exercise bench or a bench that has a seat and near-vertical back support.

Additional information: This exercise is called the military press because you should stay in an erect posture (military posture) while forcing the muscles of the arms and shoulders to do all the work. Do **not** bend or sway the back to complete a repetition.

PRESS BEHIND THE NECK

Muscles developed: Deltoid, triceps.

Starting position: Stand with a barbell resting on the top of your upper back and shoulders, your hands also supporting the bar and placed wider than shoulder-width.

Concentric phase: Inhale as you press the bar upward to arms-length overhead.

Eccentric phase: Exhale as you slowly lower the bar to the starting position.

Variations: Perform this exercise in a sitting position.

Additional information: Keep your back straight and make your arm and shoulder muscles move the weight. Do **not** lean back to complete a repetition.

UPRIGHT ROWING

Muscles developed: Deltoid, trapezius.

Starting position: Stand with a barbell hanging at arms-length in front of your body, hands in a pronated (thumbs in) grip.

Concentric phase: Inhale while pulling the elbows as high as possible in a smooth, continuous movement. The bar should reach chin level.

Eccentric phase: Exhale while slowly lowering bar to the starting position.

Additional information: Concentrate on your deltoid muscles while raising the upper arm and keeping your elbows high. The arm muscles should be as inactive as possible.

LATERAL RAISE

Muscles developed: Deltoid, trapezius.

Starting position: Stand with one dumbbell in each hand.

Concentric phase: Inhale while lifting the weights away from your body and upward. Keep your arms fairly straight, and raise the weights to shoulder level.

Eccentric phase: Exhale while lowering the weights to the starting position.

Variations: Perform the same exercise movement from a sitting position. The deltoid is a muscle with three fairly distinct parts: anterior (front), lateral (middle), and posterior (rear). The lateral raise tends to best develop the lateral part; the front raise develops the front part; and the bent-over lateral raise develops the rear part.

BENT-OVER LATERAL RAISE

Muscles developed: Posterior (rear) deltoid, rhomboids, trapezius.

Starting position: Bend over with your back flat and knees slightly bent; hold one dumbbell in each hand, arms straight, and dumbbells hanging directly below your shoulder joints.

Concentric phase: Inhale while raising the dumbbells to the side up to shoulder level. Pause briefly.

Eccentric phase: Exhale while slowly lowering the weights to the starting position.

Variations: Sit on the end of a bench or lie face down on a flat or incline bench that is high enough to allow your arms to hang fully extended.

Additional information: Lift your arms straight to the side or move them slightly forward toward your head as the weight is lifted.

FRONT RAISE

Muscles developed: Frontal deltoid, clavicular portion of pectoralis major, coracobrachialis.

Starting position: Stand and hold a barbell or two dumbbells at arms-length.

Concentric phase: Inhale while raising the weight to shoulder level, keeping your arms straight. Pause briefly.

Eccentric phase: Exhale while lowering the weight to the starting position.

Variations: Raise the weight to an overhead position, as long as you do not allow your back to arch or bend.

Note: On all straight-arm exercises some individuals feel that a slight bend at the elbow relieves unnecessary tension or strain in the elbow joint. This is no problem as long as it makes the exercise more productive for you. But do not bend your elbows to make the exercise easier for the working muscles.

UPPER ARM EXERCISES

BARBELL CURL

Muscles developed: Biceps brachii, brachialis, brachioradialis.

Starting position: Stand, holding a barbell in front of the body, hands gripping the bar at shoulder width with a supinated (thumbs out) grip.

Concentric phase: Exhale while raising the weight to your shoulders by moving only at the elbow joint.

Eccentric phase: Inhale while lowering the weight to the starting position.

Variations: Any elbow flexion or curling exercise will develop the elbow flexor muscles. Curling exercises have many variations. Vary this standing curl by changing the space between your hands when gripping the bar.

REVERSE CURL

Muscles developed: Biceps, brachialis, brachioradialis, wrist and hand flexors.

Starting position: Stand and hold a barbell in front of your body with both hands in a pronated (thumbs in) grip.

Concentric phase: Exhale while raising the bar to the shoulders by bending only at the elbows.

Eccentric phase: Inhale while lowering the bar to the starting position.

Variations: Change the distance between the hands.

Additional information: This exercise provides a strong stimulus to the forearm muscles and often is used as a forearm exercise as well as a variation of the curl.

INCLINE DUMBBELL CURL

Muscles developed: Biceps brachii, brachialis, brachiordialis.

Starting Position: With your back against an incline bench, hold one dumbbell in each hand with your arms extended and hanging directly below your shoulder joints.

Concentric phase: Exhale while bending your arms only at the elbow. Pull the weights to your shoulders.

Eccentric phase: Inhale while lowering weights to the starting position.

Variations:

1. Alternate arms so that one is coming up as the other is going down.

2. Turn the arms out so that the dumbbells are raised and lowered to the sides of the body instead of in front of the body.

SEATED DUMBBELL CURL

Muscles developed: Biceps brachii, brachialis, brachiordialis.

Starting position: Sit with your arms by your sides with one dumbbell in each hand.

Concentric phase: Exhale while bending only at your elbows to bring the weights up to your shoulders.

Eccentric phase: Inhale while lowering the weights to the starting position.

Variations:

1. Perform standing, or on an incline bench, or lying on your back on a flat bench.

2. Use several different arm positions when working with dumbbells.

3. Alternate dumbbell curls with one arm coming up while the other is going down.

UPPER ARM EXERCISES

STANDING TRICEP EXTENSION

Muscles developed: Triceps.

Starting position: Stand and hold a dumbbell overhead with both hands.

Eccentric phase: Inhale as you lower the weight behind your head.

Concentric phase: Exhale as you extend both arms and push the weight back to the starting position.

Variations:

1. Perform this exercise with a barbell.

2. Perform this exercise from a sitting position.

Additional information: Keep your elbows up throughout the exercise.

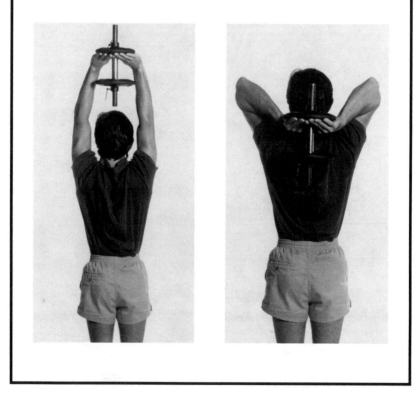

LYING TRICEP EXTENSION

Muscles developed: Triceps.

Starting positions: Lie on your back on a flat exercise bench and hold a barbell above your shoulders, with both arms straight and your hands six to eight inches apart.

Eccentric phase: Inhale while lowering the bar to the top of your forehead by bending only at your elbows.

Concentric phase: Exhale as you push the bar back to the starting position.

Variations: Perform this exercise on an incline bench or a decline bench. Use one or two dumbbells in several variations.

CLOSE-GRIP BENCH PRESS

Muscles developed: Triceps, anterior deltoid, pectoralis major.

Starting position: Lie on your back on a flat bench and hold a barbell directly above your shoulders, with your arms straight and a close grip (hands six to eight inches apart).

Eccentric phase: Inhale as you lower the bar until it touches your chest.

Concentric phase: Exhale as you press the weight back to the starting position.

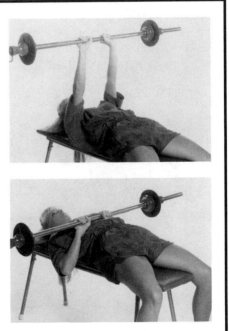

FOREARM EXERCISES

BARBELL WRIST CURL

Muscles developed: Wrist and hand flexors.

Starting positions: Sit on an exercise bench, and place your forearms on top of your thighs with your wrists just beyond your knees; hold a barbell with a supinated (thumbs out) grip, and allow the bar to hang toward the floor.

Concentric phase: Lift the weight, moving only your hands and wrists.

Eccentric phase: Slowly lower the bar to the starting position.

Variations:

1. Use one dumbbell in each hand.

2. Use one dumbbell and exercise one arm at a time.

REVERSE WRIST CURL

Muscles developed: Wrist extensors.

Starting position: Sit on an exercise bench, forearms resting on top of your thighs, wrists just beyond your knees; hold a barbell in each hand, using a pronated (thumbs in) grip.

Concentric phase: Lift the bar as high as possible, moving only at the wrist joint.

Eccentric phase: Slowly lower the bar to the starting position.

Variations:

1. Place forearms across an exercise bench.

2. Use dumbbells.

THIGH EXERCISES

SQUAT

Muscles developed: Quadriceps, gluteus maximus, hamstrings, erector spinae.

Starting position: Stand with a barbell across your shoulders and upper back.

Eccentric phase: Inhale as you bend your knees and hips while keeping your head up and your back flat. Continue bending your knees and hips until your thighs are parallel to the floor.

Concentric phase: Exhale as you straighten your legs and hips to return to a standing position.

Spotting: Have one spotter stand directly behind you, or, have one spotter at each end of the bar. If no spotters are available, use a squat rack to guarantee that you will not get stuck under a heavy weight.

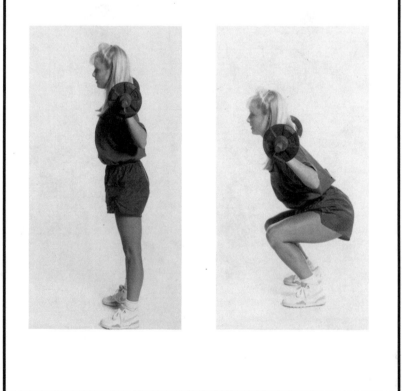

FRONT SQUAT

Muscles developed: Quadriceps, gluteus maximus, erector spinae.

Starting positions: Stand with a barbell supported across top of your chest and shoulders. Hold the bar with both hands, elbows high, at shoulder level. (One possible way to hold the bar is shown here. This method of holding the bar can be used if the bar is lifted from a rack that is about shoulder height.)

Eccentric phase: Inhale as you bend your knees and hips until your thighs are parallel to the floor.

Concentric phase: Exhale as you extend your hips and knees and return to the standing position.

Spotting: One spotter at each end of the bar would be best. If you are training alone, use a squat rack to support the weight at the bottom in case you cannot return to the standing position.

LUNGE

Muscles developed: Quadriceps, gluteus maximus.

Starting position: Assume a standing position with a dumbbell in each hand, or a barbell across your shoulders and upper back.

Eccentric phase: Inhale as you take a large step forward with one leg. Bend the knee of your forward leg, and lower your body until the thigh of the front leg is parallel to the floor. (This is essentially a one-leg parallel squat.)

Concentric phase: Exhale as you extend your forward leg, pushing yourself back to your original standing position.

Spotting: Spotting is not necessary if you are doing lunges with dumbbells. If you are doing lunges with a barbell across your back and shoulders, have one spotter stand at each end of the bar. Or perform the lunges into a squat rack that could support the weight in your lowest position in case you cannot return to the standing position.

Additional information: Try to keep your head up and upper body erect throughout the exercise.

BENCH STEP

Muscles developed: Quadriceps, gluteus maximus.

Starting position: Take a standing position with a dumbbell in each hand, or a barbell across your upper back and shoulders.

Concentric phase: Place one foot on the bench in front of you. Using your hip and leg muscles, lift yourself up until your leg is straight.

Eccentric phase: Slowly lower yourself to the starting position using the same leg.

Spotting: If using dumbbells, you should be all right without a spotter. When using a barbell, have one spotter stand behind you, and a spotter at each end of the bar. Or use a squat rack.

LEG EXERCISES

STANDING BARBELL CALF RAISE

Muscles developed: Gastrocnemius, soleus.

Starting position: Take a standing position with a barbell across your shoulders and upper back, the front half of both feet elevated so that the heels are lower than the toes.

Concentric phase: Exhale while moving only at the ankle joint to raise your heels as high as possible. Pause briefly, and completely contract the muscles on the back of your legs when you are at the highest position you can reach.

Eccentric phase: Inhale as you slowly lower both heels as far as they can go. The best stretch and maximum range of motion are achieved if your heels cannot touch the floor at the bottom position of this exercise.

Additional information: Maintaining balance is difficult during this exercise. Performing the exercise in a power rack or on a standing calf-raise machine usually increases the effectiveness of the exercise because it eliminates the balance problem.

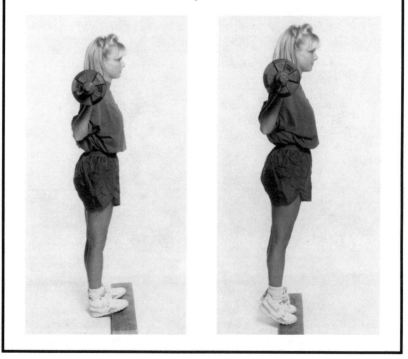

ONE-DUMBELL CALF RAISE

Muscles developed: Gastrocnemius, soleus.

Starting position: Stand with a dumbbell in one hand hanging at arms-length and resting against the side of your thigh. Place all of your body weight on the leg nearest the dumbbell and lift your other foot off the floor. Brace the free foot against the back of the support leg so that you do not use a kicking motion to help lift the weight.

Concentric phase: Exhale as you raise the heel of your support foot as high as possible. Pause at the top.

Eccentric phase: Inhale as you slowly lower the heel of your support foot to a fully stretched position.

Additional information: Place the hand that is not holding the dumbbell on a wall or some other solid support for balance. Use the support hand for balance only; do not pull with that arm to help lift the weight.

DONKEY CALF RAISE

Muscles developed: Gastrocnemius, soleus.

Starting position: Bend forward at the waist, and place your hands on an exercise bench. Position your feet so that the front half of each foot is on a raised block. Have a training partner sit on top of your hips, not on your lower back.

Concentric phase: Raise your heels as high as possible. Pause at the top.

Eccentric phase: Slowly lower your heels to a fully stretched position.

Additional information: This exercise eliminates the balance problem of standing barbell calf raises and takes the weight off of your spinal column but makes it difficult to accurately control progressive increases in resistance.

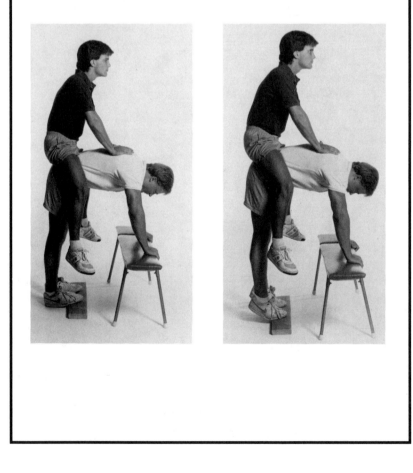

12

Weight Machine Exercises

EQUIPMENT

There are many different models of weight machines. Although they are different in design, that should not intimidate you as a beginning weight trainer. Most of the machines are safe and easy to use. Learning exercises on a weight machine is easier than using barbells and dumbbells because the machine design determines and controls the path of the exercise. When lifting barbells and dumbbells, you must control the path of the exercise movement and maintain balance. Although weight trainers generally take longer to learn to perform barbell and dumbbell exercises correctly, many experts see the additional balance learned, and the additional stabilizing muscles used, as advantages for free weights over machine weights.

Many weight machines have a stack of weight plates attached to the machine to provide the resistance. The amount of weight to be lifted is determined by the location of a selector pin that is placed between weight plates in the stack. The basic exercises — the core of any weight training program — may be performed safely without a spotter on most weight machines.

EXERCISES FOR DIFFERENT BODY PARTS

The exercises in this chapter are arranged in the following order:

Chest
Bench Press
Parallel Bar Dips

Back
Shoulder Shrug
Back Extension
Lat Pull
Pulley Rowing

Shoulders
Overhead Press
Press Behind the Neck

Upper Arm
Low Pulley Curl (elbow flexion)
Tricep Pressdown (elbow extension)

Forearm
Wrist Roller
Hand Gripper

Thigh
Leg Press
Leg Extension
Leg Curl

Leg
Calf Press
Calf Raise (bench press station)
Calf Raise (calf raise machine)

CONCENTRIC AND ECCENTRIC PHASES

The concentric and eccentric phases of a weight training exercise are explained on the first page of Chapter 11.

CHEST EXERCISES

BENCH PRESS

Muscles developed: Pectoralis major, anterior deltoid, triceps.

Starting position: Lie on your back on a flat bench; place your head toward the weight stack, with the bench press bar above your chest (you may choose to place your feet on the bench or on the floor as long as you keep your back flat on the bench throughout the exercise); on some machines you will be in a sitting position with your back against a bench.

Concentric phase: Exhale as you press the bar away from your body until your arms are fully extended.

Eccentric phase: Inhale as you allow the bar to slowly return to the starting position.

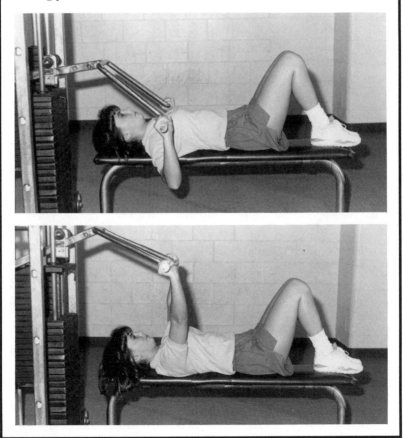

PARALLEL BAR DIPS

Muscles developed: Triceps, pectoralis major, anterior deltoid.

Starting position: Take a straight-arm support position on two bars parallel to each other and about shoulder-width apart.

Eccentric phase: Inhale as you bend your elbows and slowly lower yourself as far as possible.

Concentric phase: Exhale as you straighten your arms and return to the starting position.

Additional information: To add weight to this exercise, hang a weight or a dumbbell from a wide strap around your waist and place it between your thighs to stabilize it during the exercise.

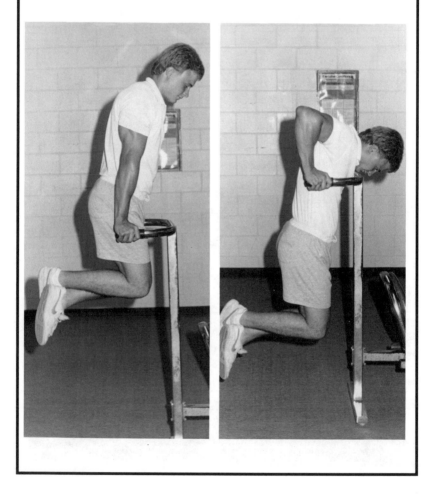

BACK EXERCISES

SHOULDER SHRUG

Muscles developed: Trapezius, levator scapulae.

Starting position: Stand at the bench press station, holding the bench press bar with a pronated (thumbs in) grip and both arms straight.

Concentric phase: Inhale as you lift or shrug your shoulders as high as possible.

Eccentric phase: Exhale as you slowly lower the weight to the starting position.

Variations:

1. Pull your shoulders forward and up, then back and down.
2. Pull your shoulders back and up, then forward and down.

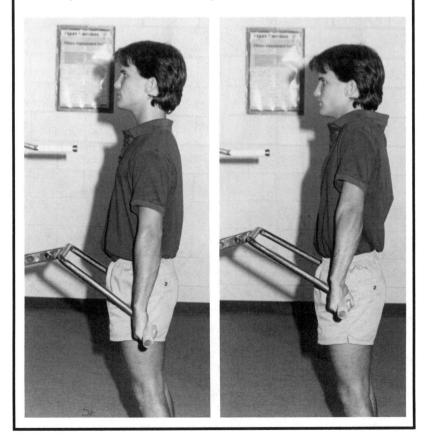

BACK EXTENSION

Muscles developed: Erector spinae.

Starting position: Assume a face-down position, with your hips supported by a back extension bench; place your feet in a position to provide stability to your legs.

Concentric phase: Inhale as you raise your upper body to a position in which your back is parallel to the floor.

Eccentric phase: Exhale as you return to the starting position.

Variations: Perform this exercise on a flat exercise bench by lying with the front of your thighs and hips on the bench and your upper body extended beyond the end of the bench. Have someone hold your feet.

Additional information: Perform this exercise with your hands placed

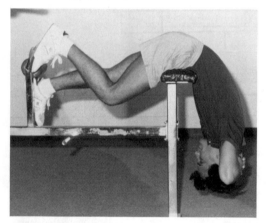

on your lower back, your arms crossed on your chest, or your hands behind your head. As your arms are moved away from your waist and toward your head, the resistance increases. To add more resistance, hold a barbell plate behind your neck or on your chest.

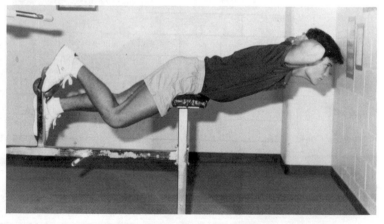

LAT PULL

Muscles developed: Latissimus dorsi, teres major, rhomboids, trapezius.

Starting position: Kneel or sit below the high pulley station and hold the exercise bar with a fairly wide grip and with both arms extended.

Concentric phase: Exhale as you pull the exercise bar to your upper back at the base of the neck.

Eccentric phase: Inhale as you return to the starting position.

Variations:

1. Pull the exercise bar to the top of your chest.

2. Alternate pulling to the front and to the back.

3. Vary the width of your hand spacing.

4. Change to a supinated (thumbs out) grip, shoulder width or closer (this is a good way to get strong enough to perform chin-ups).

Additional information: As the weight used for this exercise approaches your body weight, you might need to have someone stand behind you and hold you down by placing their hands on your shoulders near your neck.

PULLEY ROWING

Muscles developed: Latissimus dorsi, trapezius, rear deltoid, rhomboids.

Starting position: Sit on the floor in front of the low pulley station of a weight stack machine; hold the exercise bar in your hands with a pronated (thumbs in) grip.

Concentric phase: Exhale as you pull the exercise bar to the lower portion of your rib cage.

Eccentric phase: Inhale as you return to the starting position.

Variations:

1. Do this exercise in a bent-over standing position.

2. Change grip spacing or change the position on the front of the torso that the bar is pulled toward.

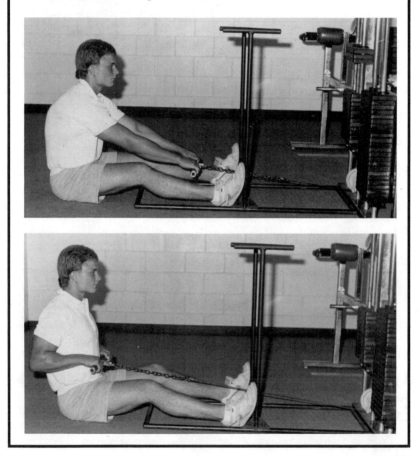

SHOULDER EXERCISES

OVERHEAD PRESS

Muscles developed: Deltoid, triceps, upper trapezius.

Starting position: Sit or stand facing the weight stack, with the exercise bar in line with your shoulders. Place your hands on the exercise bar wider than shoulder width.

Concentric phase: Inhale as you press the exercise bar upward until your arms are straight.

Eccentric phase: Exhale as you lower the exercise bar to the starting position.

Additional information: Try to keep your back straight throughout the exercise. Do *not* arch your back.

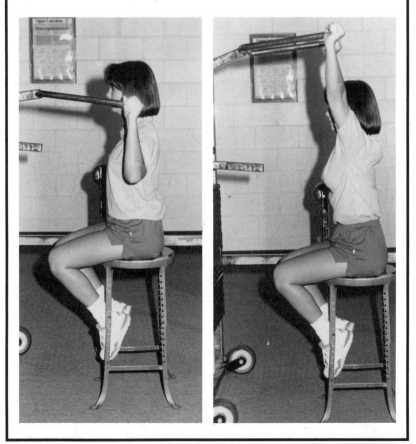

PRESS BEHIND THE NECK

Muscles developed: Deltoid, triceps, upper trapezius.

Starting position: Sit or stand facing away from the weight stack, with the exercise bar approximately in line with your shoulders. Place your hands on the bar, wider than your shoulders.

Concentric phase: Inhale as you press the exercise bar upward until your arms are straight.

Eccentric phase: Exhale as you lower the bar to the starting position.

Additional information: Try to keep your back straight during the entire exercise. Do not arch your back.

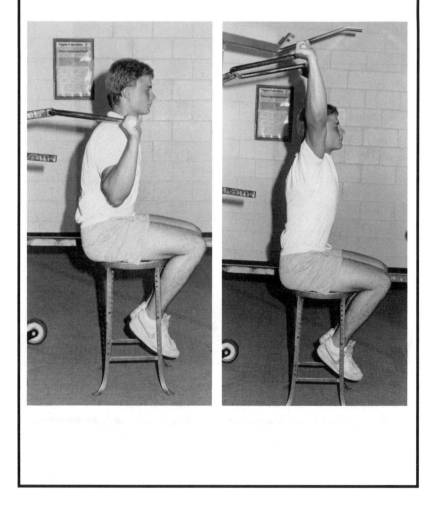

UPPER ARM EXERCISES

LOW PULLEY CURL (Elbow Flexion)

Muscles developed: Biceps brachii, brachialis, brachioradialis.

Starting position: Stand in front of the low pulley, facing the weight stack. Hold the exercise bar in a supinated (thumbs out) grip, with both arms straight.

Concentric phase: Exhale as you bend only at the elbow joint to bring the exercise bar up toward your shoulders. Move only your forearms; do not allow your upper arms to change position.

Eccentric phase: Inhale as you slowly lower the bar to the starting position.

Variations:
1. Change your grip spacing on the bar.
2. Use a pronated (thumbs in) grip and perform reverse curls.

Additional information: You can cheat on this exercise in a number of ways. Bending any joint except the elbow joint will reduce the effectiveness of the exercise.

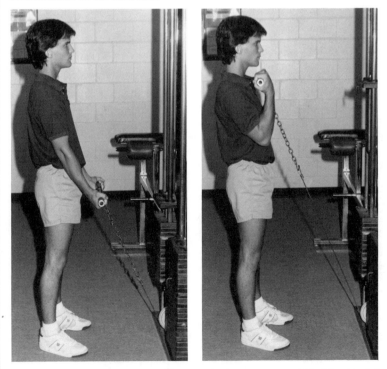

TRICEP PRESSDOWN (Elbow Extension)

Muscles developed: Triceps.

Starting position: Stand with both hands on the high pulley exercise bar in a pronated (thumbs in) grip, your hands slightly closer than shoulder width; then bring the bar down to shoulder level, with both elbows bent, and point both elbows directly toward the floor.

Concentric phase: Exhale as you press the bar down by moving only the forearms. Keep the upper arm in a fixed position throughout the exercise.

Eccentric phase: Inhale as you allow the bar to slowly return to the starting position. Do not allow your upper arm to change position.

Variations: Change the grip spacing, varying from hands together to shoulder-width apart.

Additional information: You could cheat on this exercise in a variety of ways. Be sure you keep your body still, and move only at the elbows.

FOREARM EXERCISES

WRIST ROLLER

Muscles developed: Muscles of the forearm, wrist flexors and extensors, hand flexors.

Starting position: Stand in front of the wrist roller attachment; place both hands on the wrist roller in a pronated (thumbs in) grip.

Concentric phase: Start with the wrist of one hand in full hyperextension so that the wrist is lower than the hand. Grip the wrist roller and rotate it to full flexion so the wrist is above the hand. Repeat this movement with the other hand. Continue to alternate hands until the repetitions are completed.

Variations:

1. Reverse the motion so that you start with one wrist in complete flexion (wrist above hand), and rotate the wrist roller to complete wrist hyperextension (wrist below hand).

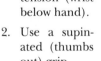

2. Use a supinated (thumbs out) grip.

HAND GRIPPER

Muscles developed: Hand flexors.

Starting position: Stand in front of the hand grip attachment; place both hands on the exercise equipment.

Concentric phase: Pull with the fingers of one hand until the gripper

cannot go farther. Pull with the fingers of the other hand until the gripper can travel no farther. Continue to alternate hands until your repetitions are completed.

Variations: Change to a supinated (thumbs out) grip.

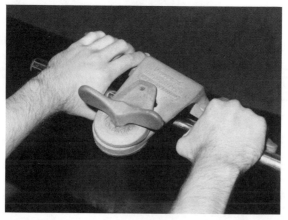

THIGH EXERCISES

LEG PRESS

Muscles developed: Quadriceps, gluteus maximus

Starting position: Sit on the leg press station; place both feet on the foot pedals. Adjust the seat to an angle of about 90° at the knee joints.

Concentric phase: Exhale as you push on the foot pedals and straighten both legs.

Eccentric phase: Inhale as you allow the weight to return to the starting position.

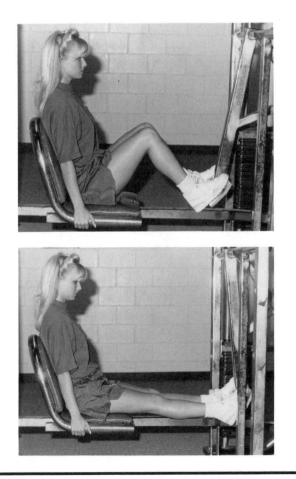

LEG EXTENSION

Muscles developed: Quadriceps.

Starting Position: Sit on the leg extension machine, with both feet behind the padded leg extension bar.

Concentric phase: Exhale as you extend both legs until they are straight.

Eccentric phase: Inhale as you allow the weight to return to the starting position.

Variations: On some leg extension machines you can perform this exercise with one leg at a time.

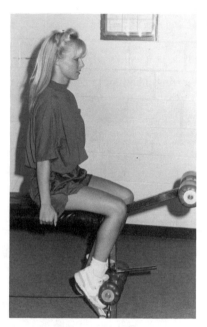

LEG CURL

Muscles developed: Hamstrings.

Starting position: Lie face down on the leg curl machine. With your legs straight, place both feet under the padded leg curl bar.

Concentric phase: Exhale as you pull both feet toward the hips, bending only at the knees.

Eccentric phase: Inhale as you allow the weight to return to the starting position.

Variations: Exercise one leg at a time.

LEG EXERCISES

CALF PRESS

Muscles developed: Gastrocnemius, soleus.

Starting position: Sit on the leg press station with both legs straight, the front half of each foot on the pedals, and the back half of each foot extending beyond the bottom of the pedals.

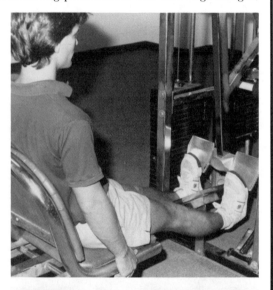

Concentric phase: Exhale as you press against the pedals with the front portion of your feet. Move only at the ankle joint.

Eccentric phase: Inhale as you allow the foot pedals to return to the starting position.

Variations:

1. Turn toes in, heels out.
2. Turn heels in, toes out.

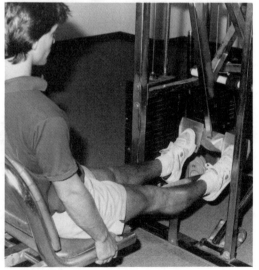

CALF RAISE (Bench Press Station)

Muscles developed: Gastrocnemius, soleus.

Starting position: Stand at the bench press station and hold the exercise bar with both hands.

Concentric phase: Exhale while raising the weight by moving only at the ankle joint.

Eccentric phase: Inhale while slowly returning to the starting position.

Variations:

1. Feet parallel.

2. Toes in.

3. Toes out.

Additional information: This exercise is more effective when the front half of the foot is placed on an elevated surface such as a block of wood.

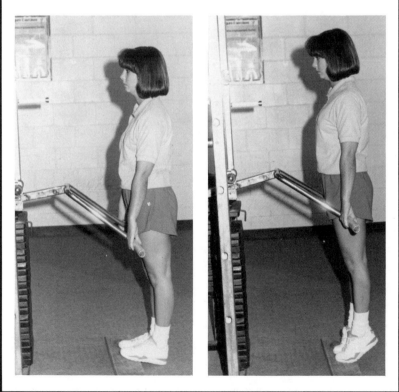

CALF RAISE (Calf Raise Machine)

Muscles developed: Gastrocnemius, soleus.

Starting position: Stand with your shoulders under the padded bars of the calf machine; place the front half of each foot on the elevated block and your heels below that level.

Concentric phase: Exhale as you raise the weight, moving only at the ankle joint.

Eccentric phase: Inhale as you return to the starting position.

Variations:

1. Feet parallel.
2. Toes in.
3. Toes out.

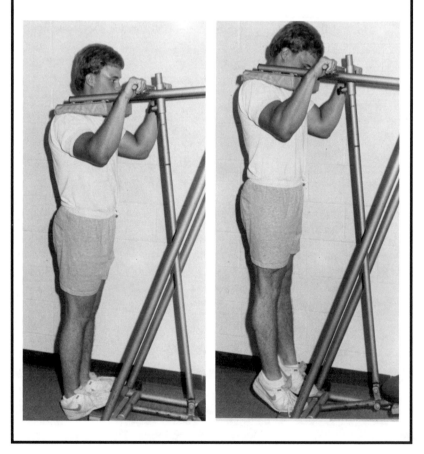

13

Abdominal Exercises

WHAT ARE ABDOMINALS AND WHY ARE THEY IMPORTANT?

The abdominal muscles cover the lower half of the front and sides of the torso. They are attached to the lower ribs of the rib cage and the upper ridges of the bones of the pelvic girdle. The abdominal muscles are not connected to the legs. Therefore, the primary actions of the abdominal muscles are trunk flexion, trunk rotation, and pulling in the abdominal contents.

The abdominal muscles include the rectus abdominis, the external obliques, the internal obliques, and the transverse abdominis. The *rectus abdominis* has vertical fibers from the lower ribs on the anterior (front) of the rib cage to the anterior part of the pelvic girdle. The primary function of the rectus abdominis is to pull the rib cage and the front of the pelvic girdle toward each other — called trunk flexion. An adequate amount of trunk flexion against resistance will strengthen the rectus abdominis.

The *external and internal obliques* have diagonal fibers connecting the ribs to the pelvic bones and to the connective tissue of the rectus abdominis. Because of their origins, insertions, and fiber direction, the oblique muscles contribute to trunk flexion and trunk rotation. An adequate amount of trunk flexion with rotation against resistance will strengthen the internal and external oblique muscles.

The *transverse abdominis* muscle also is attached to the ribs, the pelvic girdle, and the connective tissue of the rectus abdominis, but the fibers of the transverse abdominis are horizontal. The primary function of the transverse abdominis is to pull the abdominal wall inward. This muscle can be strengthened by pulling the abdominal wall inward, or back toward the spine.

Development of the abdominal muscles is important for health, appearance, and sports performance. The abdominal muscles hold the anterior part of the pelvic girdle up in its proper position, providing correct vertebral column alignment. They pull the abdominal contents inward so the lower half of the front of the torso is flat instead of bulging outward. Well developed abdominal muscles also provide the strong connection between the rib cage and the pelvic girdle that is necessary for many of the powerful torso movements required in sports performance.

The most effective abdominal exercises are those that involve trunk flexion, or trunk flexion with trunk rotation, against resistance. This can be achieved by:

1. Stabilizing the pelvic girdle and pulling the rib cage toward the pelvic girdle.

2. Stabilizing the rib cage and pulling the pelvic girdle toward the rib cage.

3. Pulling both the rib cage and the pelvic girdle toward each other.

All of these also can be done with or without trunk rotation.

Someone may tell you that you should never put your hands behind your head or neck when you are performing abdominal exercises. Actually, putting your hands behind your head is not the problem. The problem is pulling your head forward with your arms, which can result in neck injuries and neck pain. If you can perform the abdominal exercises using only your abdominal muscles and you do not pull your head forward with your arms, you may put your hands behind your head with no problem. If you catch yourself pulling your head forward with your arms, however, you should find another arm position.

EXERCISES FOR THE ABDOMINAL MUSCLES

The exercises in this chapter are arranged in the following order:

Rib Cage Toward Pelvic Girdle

Crunches, Curl-Ups
Sit-Ups
Tuck-Ups

Pelvic Girdle Toward Rib Cage

Reverse Crunches
Seated Reverse Crunches
Hanging Knee Raise

Rotation

Seated Twisting

RIB CAGE TOWARD PELVIC GIRDLE EXERCISES

CRUNCHES, CURL-UPS

Muscles developed: Rectus abdominis, abdominal obliques.

Starting position: Lie flat on your back. Bend at your knees and hips. Place your feet flat on the floor. Cross your arms over your chest, with each hand touching the opposite shoulder.

Concentric phase: Exhale as you "curl up" slowly, pulling your head, neck, shoulders, and upper back off the floor in that order. Keep your lower back on the floor throughout the exercise. At the upper limit of this movement, "crunch" the abdominal muscles by holding this fully contracted position for one or two seconds.

Eccentric phase: Slowly release the curling motion, and inhale as you return to the starting position.

(Continued on next page)

CRUNCHES, CURL-UPS (continued)

Variations:

1. Keeping your legs straight, place the back of your legs against a wall, with your hips flexed and your back on the floor.

2. Place your lower legs up on a bench with your hips and knees bent.

3. Add a twisting motion to the trunk flexion so that as you curl up, you also move one elbow toward the opposite hip. Alternate the direction of the twist on each repetition.

Additional information: If you want to add weight to this exercise, place it on the upper chest and hold it there by crossing your arms on top of the weight.

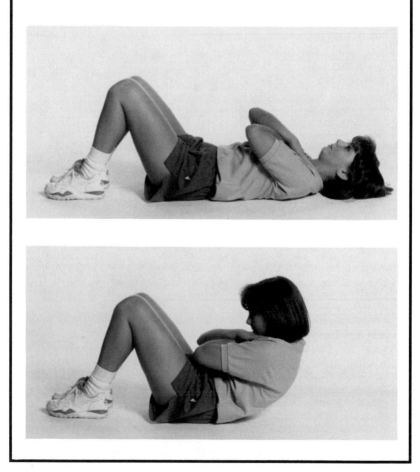

SIT-UPS

Muscles developed: Rectus abdominis, abdominal obliques.

Starting position: Lie flat on your back with your knees bent and both feet flat on the floor; place your fingertips lightly against the sides of your head.

Concentric phase: Exhale as you slowly pull your head, neck, shoulders, upper back, and lower back off the floor, in that order. *Caution:* Do *not* pull on your head with your arms.

Eccentric phase: Slowly return to the starting position by placing your lower back, upper back, shoulders, neck, and head back on the floor, in that order. Inhale as you near the starting position.

Variations:

1. Twisting sit-ups (require trunk flexion and trunk rotation). Curl up and twist, touching one elbow to the opposite knee. Alternate the direction of the twist on each repetition.

2. Change your arm position, or add weight. If you add weight, place it on your upper chest and hold it in place with your hands. As weight is added, you probably will have to anchor your feet by placing them under something or by having someone hold them.

Additional information: This exercise requires the use of the hip flexors near the end of the concentric phase of the exercise, which does not seem to be a problem if the trunk is fully flexed first. *Caution:* Do *not* pull with the hip flexor muscles until the abdominal muscles are fully contracted.

TUCK-UPS

Muscles developed: Rectus abdominis, abdominal obliques.

Starting position: Lie on your back with your legs extended and your arms extended overhead.

Concentric phase: Exhale as you flex your trunk, hips, and knees while bringing your arms and chest toward your legs. Finish in a tucked sitting position.

Eccentric phase: Inhale as you slowly return to the starting position.

Variations: The "V Sit-Up". Keep your arms and legs extended as you raise them, and touch your fingers to your toes as they reach the top of the upward motion.

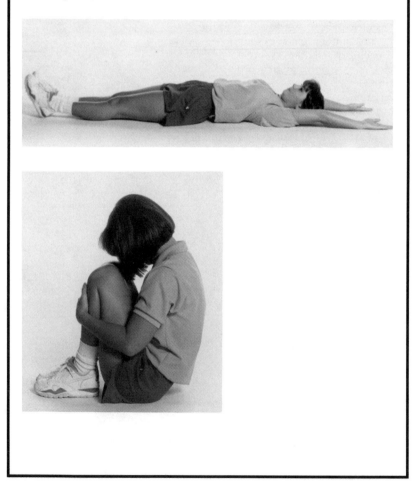

PELVIC GIRDLE TOWARD RIB CAGE EXERCISES

REVERSE CRUNCHES

Muscles developed: Rectus abdominis, abdominal obliques.

Starting position: Lie on your back, and bend your hips and knees so that your feet are flat on the floor; place your arms by your sides.

Concentric phase: Exhale as you slowly pull your knees toward your shoulders. Lift your hips and lower back off the floor. Focusing on the abdominal muscles, pull the pelvic girdle toward the rib cage. *Caution:* Do *not* roll back on your head and neck; stay on your upper back and shoulders.

Eccentric phase: Inhale as you slowly return to the starting position.

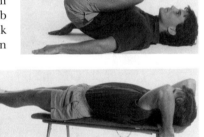

Variations:

1. Start with your legs straight. Pull your heels toward your hips first, then pull your knees toward your shoulders.

2. Twisting reverse crunches. Try to pull one knee toward the opposite shoulder. Alternate the direction of the twist on each repetition. *Caution:* Perform this exercise in a controlled manner. Vigorous twisting of the trunk can result in injury to the spinal column.

SEATED REVERSE CRUNCHES

Muscles developed: Rectus abdominis, abdominal obliques.

Starting position: Sit on the edge of a bench or chair. Lean back with your shoulders, straighten your legs, and lift both feet off of the floor.

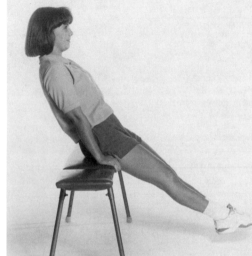

Concentric phase: Exhale as you bring your knees up toward your shoulders.

Eccentric phase: Inhale as you slowly return your legs to the starting position.

Variations:

1. Keep the hips and knees bent throughout the exercise. From this position with your legs tucked up, curl or crunch the pelvic girdle toward the rib cage, then return to the starting position but do not extend at the knee or hip joints.

2. Follow variation 1, except twist the torso so that you pull one shoulder toward the opposite knee. Alternate the twisting motion on each repetition.

HANGING KNEE RAISE

Muscles developed: Rectus abdominis, abdominal obliques, iliopsoas.

Starting position: Hang from your hands.

Concentric phase: Exhale as you bring your knees up toward your shoulders.

Eccentric phase: Inhale as you slowly return your legs to the starting position.

Variations:

1. Lift your knees up and keep them up while you do abdominal crunches.

2. Add a twisting motion near the completion of the knee raise so that one knee is pulled toward the opposite shoulder. Alternate the twisting motion on each repetition.

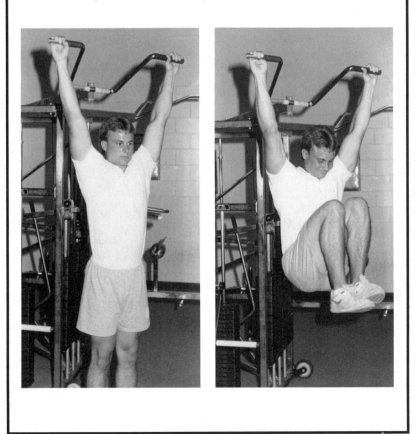

ROTATION EXERCISES

SEATED TWISTING

Muscles developed: Abdominal obliques.

Starting position: Sit on an exercise bench with a barbell on your shoulders and upper back. Straighten your arms along the bar. Place one leg on each side of a bench to stabilize your pelvic girdle.

Concentric phase: Exhale as you twist your shoulders and chest to one side. At the same time, tighten the abdominal muscles and do a crunch or curl as much as you can in a sitting position.

Eccentric phase: Inhale and straighten your back as you return to the starting position. Come to a complete stop in the starting position before twisting in the opposite direction. *Cautions:* Do *not* swing the barbell or allow it to gather momentum. Vigorous twisting can result in serious injury to the spinal column. This should be a slow, controlled exercise. Also, watch carefully for anyone walking near you so no one will get hit by the barbell.

Variations: Hold a barbell weight plate in both hands in front of your body at waist level, and perform the exercise as described.

14

Rest, Nutrition, and Drugs

REST

Weight training exercise is the stimulus, but the positive changes that occur in the muscular system as a result of weight training take place between exercise sessions as your body rebuilds and adapts to the exercise overload. Adequate rest and nutrition are necessary for these positive changes to occur.

Weight training progress is best when a muscle receives two to four days of rest between exercise sessions. Less than two days of rest or more than four days of rest between exercise sessions results in slower progress.

An average amount of sleep is eight hours per night. However, sleep requirements vary from one person to another, and for the same person based upon changes in activity levels. Beginning weight trainers initially may find they need to sleep more to recover from this new demand. As they become accustomed to the increased physical activity and their bodies begin to function more efficiently, they often return to normal sleep patterns.

"Hard gainers" — individuals who have a hard time gaining muscle — sometimes need as much as 10 hours of sleep each night. Some "easy gainers" or natural mesomorphs may gain on seven hours sleep per night. Not getting adequate rest is often one of the greatest obstacles to weight training progress for young adults.

Many high school students, college students, and young adults train hard with weights but do not get enough sleep to recover completely from their training sessions.

Weight training is intense and demanding. Too many other physical activities will slow your weight training progress. If you want to maximize your weight training gains, you should cut down on other physically strenuous activities. Young adults (ages 16 to 30) are usually the ones who wear themselves out with a large number of activities. This combination of too much activity and not enough rest can cancel out all the hard work you put into your weight training exercises.

Some experienced weight trainers believe that they progress better if they train hard for six to eight weeks, take one week off, then start a new training program.

As you get older, some of your bodily functions will naturally begin to slow down. You should not view this as a totally negative experience. Many older adults report that they need less sleep, less food, and less exercise to stay healthy and physically fit. Beyond an approximate age of 40 or 50, two weight training workouts per week might be sufficient to maintain the muscular system in excellent condition. This depends on your weight training goals and your personal ability to recover from your workouts.

Some days you feel better than others. There undoubtedly will be days when you will not feel like doing your normal workout. On those days you probably should train anyway but reduce your intensity and your total workload. You should not skip workouts completely on those days. Frequency of workouts should be maintained. Once you skip a training session, it becomes easier to skip another and another until soon you have no training schedule at all. It is easy to stop training completely and difficult to get started again. Many will begin weight training, but few will have what it takes to continue for the rest of their lives. Persistence is a common word but a rare human quality.

The only time you should not train is when you are sick or injured. If you are truly physically sick, you should not work out, because it will further stress your body. You cannot "sweat out" a cold or any other illness. Instead, you should see your doctor, follow his advice, get in bed, and rest completely so that you can get well in the shortest possible time. If you keep training, an illness can drag on for weeks, and you probably will not experience any progress in spite of your training efforts. Weight training should contribute to your health. When you are not well, you should stop training and get well, then start again. If you are sick more than two or three times a year, you should examine your lifestyle.

If you feel exhausted when you wake up and are sleepy all day long, even during activities you normally enjoy, you may not be getting enough rest. If you are sleeping about eight hours each night but are still feeling tired, you may be overtraining. In that case, you might try reducing the total number of sets in your weight training program and see if you feel better.

Adequate rest and recovery time are essential to your weight training progress.

NUTRITION

The six classes of nutrients that your body needs to function properly are:

1. Water.
2. Minerals.
3. Vitamins.
4. Carbohydrates.
5. Fats.
6. Proteins.

Water

Water contains no calories or vitamins, yet it is essential, in relatively large quantities, for the human body to function properly. When you are thirsty, your body is asking for water. What do you give it?

Thirst is not always an accurate indication of your need for water. It is recommended that every person drink at least 8 to 10 glasses of water a day. But factors such as your size, activity level, environment, and diet affect your need for water.

You would have difficulty drinking too much water. If you do take in more water than you need, your body can easily get rid of the excess. If you do not take in enough water, your body cannot continue to function normally and your performance will suffer.

Minerals

Minerals are inorganic substances that are necessary for some of the chemical activity that goes on in your body. If the appropriate minerals are not present, certain chemical changes cannot occur. Therefore, an adequate mineral intake is desirable, but more is not better.

Vitamins

Vitamins are organic substances that are necessary for some of the chemical activity that goes on in your body. They are necessary for tissue building, releasing energy, and controlling the body's use of food.

The two major categories of vitamins are: *fat-soluble* (A,D,E,K) and *water soluble* (all others). Fat-soluble vitamins can be stored in your body, and you can take in too much of these fat-soluble vitamins. Excess water-soluble vitamins normally are excreted in the urine. A toxic effect can occur when certain vitamins are taken in excessive amounts.

Your body needs adequate amounts of water, minerals, and vitamins. In each case, a deficiency will decrease optimal bodily function and performance. More than the required amount, however, will not improve performance or progress. A good guideline to follow is to eat a balanced diet from a variety of good foods and to drink at least 8 to 10 glasses of water a day.

Carbohydrates and Fiber

Calories (body fuel) are contained in carbohydrates, fats, and proteins. Carbohydrates are a major source of energy for your body, particularly during high-intensity exercise. Carbohydrates are classified into simple and complex carbohydrates.

Simple carbohydrates, frequently called simple sugars, tend to have little nutritive value. Foods such as cookies, soft drinks, and candy are high in simple sugars and often take the place of more nutritious foods.

Complex carbohydrates provide the body with many of the valuable nutrients needed to stay healthy. Major sources of complex carbohydrates are breads, fruits, vegetables, dairy products, and cereals.

Complex carbohydrates also can be an excellent source of fiber. Fiber is a type of complex carbohydrate that comes from plants. Although the human body cannot digest fiber, an adequate intake of dietary fiber is associated with several health benefits.

Fats

Fats have a higher energy value than carbohydrates, providing up to 70% of your total body energy when you are in a resting state or during low-level physical activity. Fats also are an essential component of cell walls and nerve fibers. Fats are involved in absorbing and transporting fat-soluble vitamins.

Although fats are useful in your body, it is possible to have too much of a good thing. What you need is the right amount of fat in your diet. The recommended amount is less than 30% of your total daily calories. Fats should not be cut out of your diet completely, but you should not eat too many fats. Either extreme can be detrimental.

Although there are several different categories of fats, one category, saturated fats, requires mention because of the associated risk of cardiovascular disease. Saturated fats contribute to an increase in blood cholesterol levels. Elevated blood cholesterol is a major risk factor for heart disease. Less than 10% of your total daily caloric intake should come from saturated fats.

Proteins

Proteins are complex organic compounds made up of amino acids. They are essential for growth and repair of your body tissues. Proteins are a potential source of energy but normally are not used for fuel when carbohydrates and fats are available.

Of the 22 amino acids that have been identified, nine are essential in your diet. If any one of the amino acids is missing, your body cannot put together all of the protein structures it needs. This includes muscle tissue.

Carbohydrates, fats, and proteins are all necessary in your food intake. In each case, a deficiency creates a problem, an adequate amount is optimal, and more is not better. The suggested caloric intake balance for adults is:

55%-60% carbohydrates
Less than 30% fats
10%-20% proteins

The 'Secret' Weight Training Diet

Many weight trainers and athletes are looking for the "secret" or "magic" diet that will make them successful. The truth is that no one food or special diet can do that. The closest thing to a secret or magic diet is a balanced diet that includes all the nutrients your body needs in the correct amounts.

The only major difference between the diet that is best for the average sedentary adult and the diet that is best for the active athlete or weight trainer is the total number of calories consumed. The athlete or weight trainer may use more total calories because of greater energy expenditure.

The "secret" weight training diet should include a wide variety of good quality food in the proper amounts. You must eat right to gain healthy muscle tissue and remove excess stored body fat. Carbonated drinks and chips will not produce quality muscle tissue but certainly can be stored as fat. Get the junk food out of your diet and eat high quality food — learn to tell the difference. Some of the top body builders in the world claim that their body building success is 80% nutrition and 20% training.

One relatively easy way to balance all of the complex nutritional requirements is to follow this simple food group plan (also see Figure 14.1 on pages 157-158):

Grain products   4 servings per day
(breads and cereals)

Fruits and vegetables   4 servings per day

Meat: 2 servings per day
(protein from plant sources provide
lower fat intake while increasing
carbohydrate and fiber intake)

Milk   2 servings per day
(dairy products)

Junk food   0 servings per day

Food Supplements

When you are eating a balanced diet of good quality foods, you don't need food supplements. No miracle food or magic food will make your muscles grow. Independent researchers (those who don't sell food supplements) have found that no benefit results from protein supplements or vitamin supplements when subjects are on a balanced diet.

Weight Gain

To gain muscular body weight, you should perform brief but heavy weight training exercise, work the largest muscle groups, and eat a balanced diet of high quality food. Your total caloric intake should increase by 500 to 1,000 calories per day. You should eat more frequently, but eat smaller meals, and get plenty of rest. Slow down, stay calm, and decrease your other activities.

Weight Loss

When you start a weight training program, you will gain muscle and lose fat. Any significant loss in total body weight is difficult to attain until muscle growth slows down. To lose excess body fat, you should perform longer training sessions consisting of more sets, repetitions, and exercises, which will use more total calories. Continuous, rhythmic activities that use large muscle groups are best for high caloric expenditure. Examples of good fat-loss activities are walking, swimming, cycling, and jogging.

The "secret" is to:

- Eat a balanced diet of good quality food.

- Do not skip meals or omit any particular food group.

- Decrease your total caloric intake by 500 to 1,000 calories per day.

- Participate in more physical activities, and select activities in which food is not easily available.

- Try getting less rest and sleep. Caloric expenditure is generally lowest when you are resting and sleeping.

DRUGS, ALCOHOL, AND TOBACCO

Anabolic Steroids

Anabolic steroids present the biggest drug problem in weight training. They are synthetic compounds that are like the natural hormones your body produces. Anabolic steroids are thought to promote muscular growth, but they have been difficult to study because they produce highly undesirable and dangerous side effects. Therefore, they can be studied only at safe (low) levels. The athletes who claim that steroids work take massive doses, 10 to 20

GUIDE TO GOOD EATING

Every day eat a wide variety of foods from the Four Food Groups in moderation.

Milk Group

Supplies many nutrients including:
- calcium
- protein
- riboflavin

2 servings for adults
3 servings for children
4 servings for teenagers and pregnant or breastfeeding women

Meat Group

Supplies many nutrients including:
- protein
- iron
- niacin
- thiamin

2 servings for all ages
3 servings for pregnant women

Fruit-Vegetable Group

Supplies many nutrients including:
- vitamin A
- vitamin C

4 servings for all ages

Grain Group

Supplies many nutrients including:
- carbohydrate
- iron
- thiamin
- niacin

4 servings for all ages

Combination Foods

Combination Foods are made up of foods from more than one food group. Therefore, they supply the same nutrients as the foods they contain.

"Others" Category

Foods in the "Others" category are often high in calories and/or low in nutrients. They don't take the place of foods from the Four Food Groups in supplying nutrients.

Condiments
Barbeque sauce
Catsup, mustard
Olives, pickles
Salt
Soy sauce

Chips and Related Products
Corn chips
Popcorn
Potato chips
Pretzels
Tortilla chips

Fats and Oils
Coffee whitener
Cream, sour cream
Gravy, cream sauce
Margarine, butter
Mayonnaise
Oil, lard, shortening
Salad dressing

Sweets
Brownies, cookies
Cakes, pies
Candy
Jelly, jam
Sugar, honey, syrup
Sweet rolls, doughnuts

Alcohol
Beer
Gin, vodka
Whiskey, rum
Wine

Other Beverages
Coffee, tea
Fruit-flavored drinks
Soft drinks

0001N ☐ 1989. Copyright © 1989, 5th Edition. NATIONAL DAIRY COUNCIL, Rosemont, IL 60018-4233. All rights reserved. Printed in U.S.A.

ISBN 1-55647-001-0

Guide to Good Eating courtesy of NATIONAL DAIRY COUNCIL®

Figure 14.1. Guide to Good Eating.

times greater than the safe dose a physician would allow in a research study. Some of the undesirable side effects that have been observed are: endocrine disturbances, atrophy of the testicles, male impotency, liver damage, liver cancer, and coronary artery disease.

All steroid users agree that steroids work only when accompanied by extremely hard weight training. Therefore, steroids are not an "easy gain" muscle drug that replaces hard work. Intense workouts are necessary. This is another reason why steroids are hard to research and study. It is difficult to determine how much of the improvement is a result of the extremely hard training and how much can be attributed to the steroid effect.

Many steroid users report an increase in aggressiveness. This increased aggressiveness during weight training workouts could result in more intense workouts and greater gains by itself. At any rate, however, anabolic steroids do not have proven value in increasing weight training progress and do have dangerous side effects. The use of steroids will also result in disqualification from top-level lifting competitions.

Some young lifters and body builders who are taking steroids are causing lifelong damage to their bodies. Steroid abuse has also caused a number of deaths of young men.

Weight training is an activity that should improve your health and natural performance level. Drug abuse has no place in a health development program such as weight training.

Alcohol

There is no evidence that a low level of alcohol consumption interferes with weight training progress. In contrast, heavy alcohol consumption has a profound and obvious detrimental effect on the human body.

Tobacco

Smoking or chewing tobacco has no known beneficial effects. Smoking is harmful to the respiratory and circulatory systems. It decreases a person's performance capability and training capacity. Smoking reduces the ability to complete demanding weight training workouts and also interferes with the ability to recover from workouts.

References and Suggested Readings

Allsen, Philip E. *Strength Training: Beginners, Bodybuilders, and Athletes.* Glenview, IL: Scott, Foresman and Company, 1987.

Alter, Michael J. *The Science of Stretching.* Champaign, IL: Human Kinetics Books, 1988.

Anderson, Bob. *Stretching.* Bolinas, CA: Shelter Publications, 1980.

Berger, Richard A. *Introduction to Weight Training.* Englewood Cliffs, NJ: Prentice Hall, 1984.

Brooks, George A., and Thomas D. Fahey. *Exercise Physiology: Human Bioenergetics and Its Applications.* New York: Macmillan Publishing Company, 1985.

Brooks, George A., and Thomas D. Fahey. *Fundamentals of Human Performance.* New York: Macmillan Publishing Company, 1987.

Cook, Brian, and Gordon W. Stewart. *Get Strong: A Sensible Guide to Strength Training for Fitness and Sports.* Santa Barbara, CA: 3 S Fitness Group, 1981.

deVries, Herbert A. *Physiology of Exercise For Physical Education and Athletics.* Dubuque, IA: Wm. C. Brown Publishers, 1986.

Epley, Boyd. *Dynamic Strength Training for Athletes.* Dubuque, IA: Wm. C Brown Publishers, 1985.

Epley, Boyd, and Tom Wilson. *Weight Training Instruction Manual.* Lincoln, NE: Body Enterprises, 1981.

Fahey, Thomas D. *Basic Weight Training.* Mountain View, CA: Mayfield Publishing Company, 1989.

Ferrigno, Lou, and Douglas Kent Hall. *The Incredible Lou Ferrigno.* New York: Simon and Schuster, 1982.

Fleck, Steven J., and William J. Kraemer. *Designing Resistance Training Programs.* Champaign, IL: Human Kinetics Books, 1987.

Fox, Edward L. *Sports Physiology.* Philadelphia: Saunders College Publishing, 1984.

Fox, Edward L., Richard W. Bowers, and Merle L. Foss. *The Physiological Basis of Physical Education and Athletics.* Philadelphia: Saunders College Publishing, 1988.

Grant, Norman G. *Resistive Weight Training.* Dubuque, IA: Kendall-Hunt Publishing Company, 1986.

Hatfield, Frederick C., and March Krotee. *Personalized Weight Training for Fitness and Athletics.* Dubuque, IA: Kendall-Hunt Publishing Company, 1984.

Hesson, James. *A Formula for Success.* Unpublished research material, 1980.

Hoeger, Werner W. K. *Principles and Labs for Physical Fitness and Wellness.* Englewood, CO: Morton Publishing Company, 1991.

Johnson, Maurice. *Weight Lifting and Conditioning Exercises.* Dubuque, IA: Eddie Bowers Publishing Company, 1989.

Lamb, David R. *Physiology of Exercise: Responses and Adaptations.* New York: Macmillan Publishing Company, 1984.

Lombardi, V. Patterson. *Beginning Weight Training.* Dubuque, IA: Wm. C. Brown Publishers, 1989.

McArdle, William D., Frank I. Katch, and Victor L. Katch. *Exercise Physiology: Energy, Nutrition and Human Performance.* Philadelphia: Lea and Febiger, 1986.

McHugh, Thomas P. *Weight Training for Fitness and Sports.* Dubuque, IA: Kendall-Hunt Publishing Company, 1984.

Moran, Gary, and George McGlynn. *Dynamics of Strength Training.* Dubuque, IA: Wm. C. Brown Publishers, 1990.

National Strength and Conditioning Association. *Position Paper on Prepubescent Strength Training.* Lincoln, NE: NSCA, 1985.

National Strength and Conditioning Association. *Position Paper on Strength Training for Female Athletes.* Lincoln, NE: NSCA, 1990.

Noble, Bruce J. *Physiology of Exercise and Sport.* St. Louis: Times Mirror/Mosby College Publishing, 1986.

O'Shea, John P. *Scientific Principles and Methods of Strength Fitness.* Reading, MA: Addison-Wesley Publishing Company, 1976.

Powers, Scott K., and Edward T. Howley. *Exercise Physiology: Theory and Application to Fitness and Performance.* Dubuque, IA: Wm. C. Brown Publishers, 1990.

Rasch, Philip J. *Weight Training.* Dubuque, IA: Wm. C. Brown Publishers, 1990.

Riley, Daniel P. *Strength Training by the Experts.* West Point, NY: Leisure Press, 1982.

Riley, Daniel P., and James A. Peterson. *Not for Men Only: Strength Training for Women.* West Point, NY: Leisure Press, 1981.

Sienna, Phillip A. *One Rep Max: A Guide to Beginning Weight Training.* Indianapolis, IN: Benchmark Press, 1989.

Sprague, Ken, and Bill Reynolds. *The Golds Gym Book of Bodybuilding.* Chicago: Contemporary Books, 1983.

Stone, Michael, and Harold O'Bryant. *Weight Training: A Scientific Approach.* Minneapolis: Burgess International Group, 1987.

Stone, William J., and William A. Kroll. *Sports Conditioning and Weight Training.* Boston: Allyn and Bacon, 1986.

Thomas, Tom R. *Muscular Fitness Through Resistance Training.* Dubuque, IA: Eddie Bowers Publishing Company, 1986.

Tuten, Rich, Clancy Moore, and Virgil Knight. *Weight Training Everyone.* Winston-Salem, NC: Hunter Textbooks, 1986.

Westcott, Wayne L. *Strength Fitness: Physiological Principles and Training Techniques.* Dubuque, IA: Wm. C. Brown Publishing, 1989.

Wilmore, Jack H., and David L. Costill. *Training For Sport and Activity.* Dubuque, IA: Wm. C. Brown Publishers, 1988.

APPENDIX A

Muscle Structure

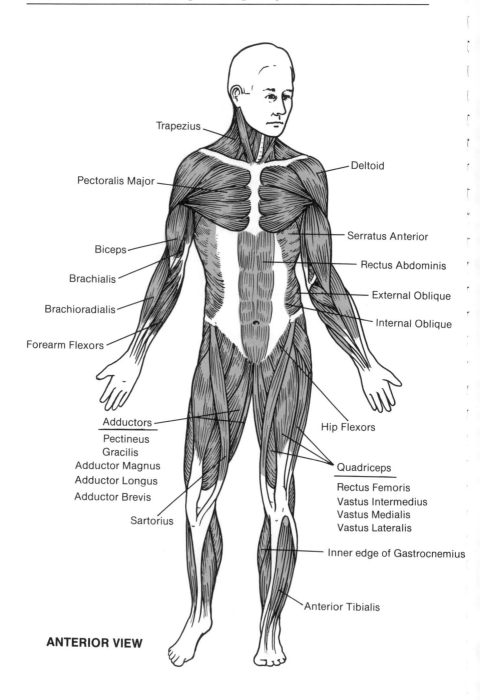

Trapezius

Deltoid

Pectoralis Major

Serratus Anterior

Biceps

Rectus Abdominis

Brachialis

External Oblique

Brachioradialis

Internal Oblique

Forearm Flexors

Adductors
Pectineus
Gracilis
Adductor Magnus
Adductor Longus
Adductor Brevis

Hip Flexors

Quadriceps
Rectus Femoris
Vastus Intermedius
Vastus Medialis
Vastus Lateralis

Sartorius

Inner edge of Gastrocnemius

Anterior Tibialis

ANTERIOR VIEW

Figure A.1. Major muscles of the human body (anterior view).

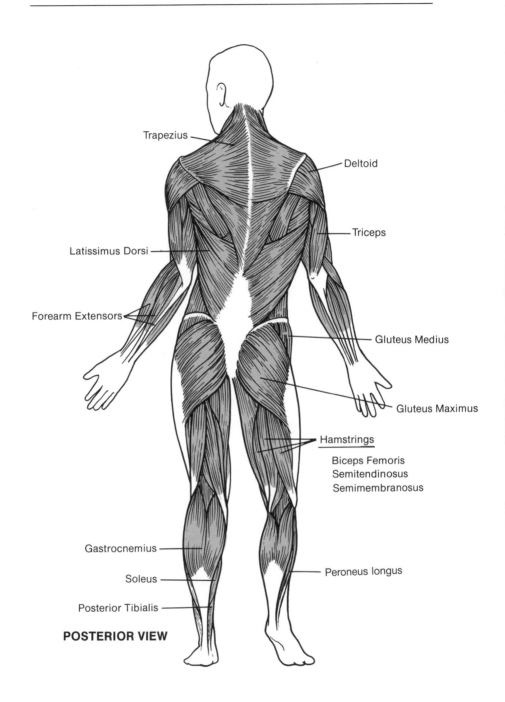

Figure A.1. Major muscles of the human body (posterior view).

APPENDIX B

Forms

Name _____

Section _____

Goal Setting

Directions:

1. Read Chapter 7, "A Formula for Success."
2. Make your weight training goals specific, measurable, believable, and compatible.
3. Set a specific date by which you will reach your goal.
4. Make the goals **your** goals, something you want very much. The greater your desire for the goal, the greater is your chance of achieving it.
5. Include changes in muscular strength, size, or endurance.
6. Write at least one, but not more than three, personal weight training goals. These should be short-term goals that can be reached in the next three months.

Goal 1: _____

_____

_____

_____

_____

Goal 2: _____

_____

_____

_____

_____

Goal 3: _____

_____

_____

_____

_____

Name ————————————————————————————

Section ——————————————————————————

Planning Your Personal
Weight Training Program

Directions:

1. Read Chapter 9, "Planning a Weight Training Program."
2. Plan an exercise program that is consistent with your goals.
3. Refer to Chapters 11, 12, and 13 for specific exercises.

General Body Part	Specific Exercise	Resistance % of 1-RM	Repetitions	Sets	Rest Interval	Frequency Days/wk.

Name _____

Section _____

Size Measurement

Directions:

1. Read Chapter 8, "Record Keeping and Progress."

		1st Measurement Date:		2nd Measurement Date:		3rd Measurement Date:		4th Measurement Date:	
Height									
Weight									
Neck	(relaxed)								
Shoulders	(relaxed)								
Chest	(relaxed)								
	(flexed)								
Waist	(relaxed)								
	(flexed)								
Hips	(relaxed)								
	(flexed)								
Right (r) Left (L)		R	L	R	L	R	L	R	L
Thigh	(relaxed)								
	(flexed)								
Calf	(relaxed)								
	(flexed)								
Upper Arm	(relaxed)								
	(flexed)								
Forearm	(relaxed)								
	(flexed)								

Name _____

Section _____

Strength Measurement

Directions:

1. Read Chapter 8, "Record Keeping and Progress."
2. Train with weights for at least two weeks before testing strength.
3. Test your strength every three or four weeks after the first test.
4. Move the weight in a smooth, continuous manner.
5. Maintain strict exercise form.
6. Do **not** hold your breath.
7. Increase the weight for each set.
8. Rest between sets.
9. Rest three to five minutes before your final record attempt.
10. Start with a light weight that you can lift 10 times. After that first warm-up set, continue raising the weight and performing one repetition until you reach your one-repetition maximum (1-RM). Try to reach your 1-RM within five or six total sets.

Strength Test	1st Test	2nd Test	3rd Test	4th Test
	Date:	Date:	Date:	Date:
Exercise:	Wt	Wt	Wt	Wt

Name ——————————————————————————————

Section ——————————————————————————————

Muscle Endurance Measurement

Directions:

1. Read Chapter 8, "Record Keeping and Progress."
2. Test your strength to find your one-repetition maximum.
3. Select a weight that is approximately 60% of your 1-RM.
4. Perform as many continuous repetitions as possible, with absolutely **no** rest pause between repetitions.
5. Move the weight in a smooth, controlled manner.
6. Maintain strict exercise form.
7. Test your muscle endurance every three or four weeks after the first test.
8. Use the same weight for each exercise every time you test yourself for muscle endurance on that exercise. An increase in repetitions using the same weight should indicate an increase in muscle endurance.

Muscle Endurance Test		1st Test Date:	2nd Test Date:	3rd Test Date:	4th Test Date:
Exercise	Weight	Reps	Reps	Reps	Reps

Name _____

Section _____

Date												
Exercise	Wt	Rep	Wt	Rep	Wt	Rep	Wt	Rep	Wt	Rep	Wt	Rep

Name

Section

Date												
Exercise	Wt	Rep	Wt	Rep	Wt	Rep	Wt	Rep	Wt	Rep	Wt	Rep

Name _____

Section _____

Date												
Exercise	**Wt**	**Rep**	**Wt**	**Rep**	**Wt**	**Rep**	**Wt**	**Rep**	**Wt**	**Rep**	**Wt**	**Rep**

Name _____

Section _____

Date												
Exercise	**Wt**	**Rep**	**Wt**	**Rep**	**Wt**	**Rep**	**Wt**	**Rep**	**Wt**	**Rep**	**Wt**	**Rep**

Name _____

Section _____

Date												
Exercise	**Wt**	**Rep**	**Wt**	**Rep**	**Wt**	**Rep**	**Wt**	**Rep**	**Wt**	**Rep**	**Wt**	**Rep**

Name _____

Section _____

Date												
Exercise	Wt	Rep	Wt	Rep	Wt	Rep	Wt	Rep	Wt	Rep	Wt	Rep

Name _____

Section _____

Date												
Exercise	Wt	Rep	Wt	Rep	Wt	Rep	Wt	Rep	Wt	Rep	Wt	Rep

Name _____

Section _____

Date												
Exercise	Wt	Rep	Wt	Rep	Wt	Rep	Wt	Rep	Wt	Rep	Wt	Rep

Index